BRYCE GUIDES

MW00426512

I-5 Travel Guide

Washington

A comprehensive guide to services and attractions along
Interstate 5

Ed and Carolyn Bryce

Bryce Publications
Federal Way, Washington

This book can be ordered directly from the publisher:

Bryce Publications
P.O. Box 23365
Federal Way, Wa 98093-0365
1-800-662-1437

Send $14.95 ($18.95 Canadian) plus $2.00 postage and handling for the first book, $1.00 for each additional book. (Washington residents add $1.23 per book for State sales tax.) For terms for volume quantities, please contact the publisher.

For Steven...
who rode along

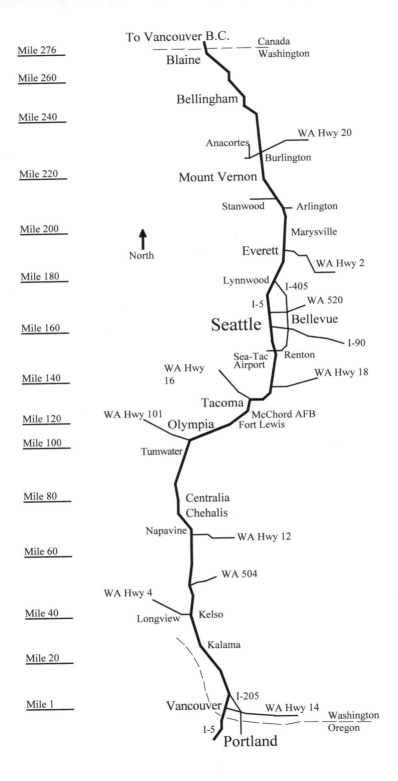

How to Use This Guide

This Guide is written for those of you who find yourself driving along I-5 and..

..want to stop for an ice cream cone or a good meal...

..are ready to stop for the night and want to find a motel that will let you bring your pet poodle in with you...

..want to give the kids a chance to get out and run around for a little while...

..have car trouble at 2:00 a.m. and need a mechanic.. fast...

..forgot to bring cat food or need to find a vet.

This book is also for those of you who commute on I-5. It contains maps that show how side roads run from exit to exit so that you can get off and go around when traffic is backed up. (If you live in Seattle or Tacoma, you KNOW what we mean....)

We start at the southern border in Vancouver, Washington, and go north to the Canadian border. Exits are numbered by the State Highway department to correspond with mileage from the Oregon border. For example, at Exit 252, you are 252 miles north of Oregon.

We've discovered a few tips while doing our research. For example:

..Always inquire about discounts when you stop at a hotel! Most hotels offer discounts, but they won't tell you about them if you don't ask.

..Lots of hotels offer breakfast with the price of the room. Those hotels can be pretty good deals - especially if you're traveling with a family.

..If you're traveling with kids, look for family suites. Rooms with a couple of bedrooms often cost less than separate rooms.

Hotel rates vary quite a bit from season to season. We've tried to give you an idea of average hotel prices, but they might be slightly different when you get there, depending on when you're traveling.

You might wonder about some of our categories. For example, we've put some chain restaurants that always have the same format and menu, such as Denny's and Shari's, in the fast-food category, even though they provide sit-down, full service. We did that in order to save space, so we wouldn't have to copy the same description over and over.

Be sure to use the Index. It will save time when you're looking for something specific. We've divided it into categories like *Fast Food* and *Lodging* to help you find what you need more quickly.

Some of the road signs are a little different a mile or two ahead of the exit than they are when you get to the exit itself. We're describing the signs as they appear right at the exit.

We've done our best to check and recheck the maps and features we're describing, but we were amazed at how quickly things changed as we were writing. For example, when we returned to proof our book, some gas stations were completely leveled and all traces gone. Only an empty lot remained. So you might occasionally be disappointed. But use the Index. It should help you find replacement services in no time. And call ahead. We've included telephone numbers for most hotels and many other locations.

If you find places you especially like, or additions or corrections we should make, please write and tell us! We'd love to hear from you, and we'll use your feedback in our next edition.

We had a good time researching and writing this book. We hope you'll get as much enjoyment from using it as we have from preparing it for you. Enjoy!

Symbols

In this edition, we use the following symbols:

HOTELS:
☺	Serviceable
☺☺	Nice
☺☺☺	Luxury

RESTAURANTS:
$	Less than $5 per person for dinner
$$	$5 - $15 per person for dinner
$$$	$15 - $25 per person for dinner
$$$$	More than $25 per person for dinner

MAP SYMBOLS:
▯	Stop light	⟶	
Ⓢ	Cash machine	one-way street	

On further reflection, we will probably change our system of rating in the next edition. For example, we found that three ☺'s don't provide enough of a range to adequately describe the variety in the comfort and amenities provided by different hotels. We also found that although many restaurants qualify for a $ for breakfast and lunch, very few, if any, offer dinner in that price range.

Exit 1A

There are no services at this exit. It is the intersection of State Highway 14 and Interstate 5.

Key Features: No services.

Northbound: Southbound:

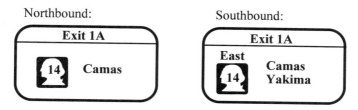

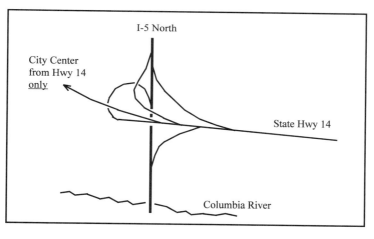

The next few exits provide access to Vancouver, WA. Vancouver is a lovely city overlooking the Columbia River and Portland, OR, across the river. If you're ready for a stop, try Exit 1B and visit Fort Vancouver. There are plenty of places to eat or spend the night nearby, all readily accessible from any of the Vancouver exits.

Exit 1B

This exit is *Northbound* only. It is closely tied to Exits 1C and 1D via Main Street, C Street, and Fort Vancouver Way. See Exits 1C and 1D for additional services that you can reach easily from this exit. If you want to go North on I-5, you must drive to Exit 1C or 1D for a Northbound entrance.

Key Features: Food, lodging, Greyhound bus depot, and a large city park.

Towing:
Vancouver Towing 696-0441
Chappelle's Towing 696-1710

Exit 1B

City Center
6th Street

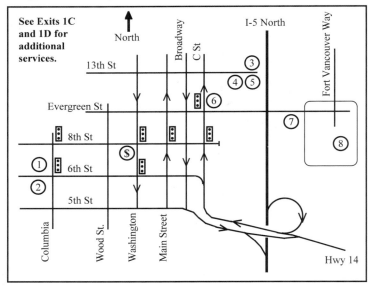

Restaurants

(5) CATTLE COMPANY $$
11am-4pm Mon-Fri (lunch), 4pm-10pm Sun-Thur, 4pm-10:30pm Fri-Sat. Full-service Stuart Anderson restaurant featuring an American menu specializing in steak. Cash & credit cards. Full bar & good food in a quiet atmosphere. This is a good place to stop to unwind.

(6) EL PRESIDENTE MEXICAN RESTAURANT & CANTINA $$
11am-2am, 7 days. Full-service restaurant with take-out available, featuring a Mexican menu. Cash & credit cards & checks. Full bar.

Restaurant is in the historic, remodeled Century House. Mariachi band on Fri, Sat, and Sun nights.

Lodging

(3) FORT MOTEL   ☺ $$
(206) 694-3327 Non-smoking rooms available. Some rooms have kitchenettes. Cash & credit cards. Phones, cable TV. Pets OK. Discounts, weekly rates available. Guest laundry, snacks in the lobby. Friendly people. A real bargain in the heart of downtown Vancouver.

Exit 1B *continued*

④ SHILO INN ☺☺☺ $$$
1-800-222-2244, local: 696-3233
Non-smoking & handicapped
rooms available. Some rooms
have kitchenettes. Cash & credit
cards & checks. Phones, cable
TV. Pets OK with fee. Elevators.
Discounts & weekly rates
available. Guest laundry,
seasonal outdoor pool, spa, steam
room, sauna. Shuttle service to
Portland Airport & Amtrack
station. Free video tapes,
newspapers, & continental
breakfast in lobby.

Other

① CITY PARK
   Historic Chas. Slonim house,
   locomotive, restrooms
② GREYHOUND BUS DEPOT
⑦ STATE PATROL
⑧ FORT VANCOUVER
   Officer's Row: Offices and
   shops in picturesque,
   restored Army officers'
   quarters.
   Old Fort Vancouver:
   Visitor center and museum,
   open 9am-4pm daily; park
   with picnic tables and
   magnificent view of the
   Columbia River.
   Pearson Air Museum:
   Oldest operating airfield in
   U.S., open noon-5pm Wed-
   Sun, closed Mon-Tues.

Exit 1C

This exit provides quick access to the heart of downtown Vancouver, Clark County College, the Clark County Museum, gas, and food. It is closely tied to Exits 1B and 1D via Main St., C St., and Fort Vancouver Way. See Exits 1B and 1D for additional services that you can reach easily from this exit.

Key Features: Downtown Vancouver

Towing: Vancouver Towing 696-0441; Chappelle's Towing 696-1710

Northbound:

Exit 1C
Mill Plain Blvd

Southbound:

Exit 1C
Mill Plain Blvd **City Center**

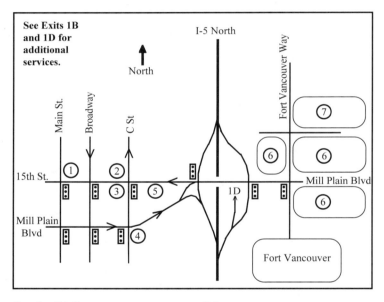

See Exits 1B and 1D for additional services.

Service Stations

③ **CHEVRON** 6:30am-8pm Mon-Fri, 8am-6pm Sat, 9am-6pm Sun. Self-serve, phone, cash & credit cards, no restrooms.

Fast Food

④ **BURGERVILLE**
⑤ **DENNY'S**

Other

① **CLARK COUNTY MUSEUM** Open 1pm-5pm Tue-Sun, Historical Society, research library on genealogy & the railroad.
② **CAR WASH**
⑥ **VANCOUVER CENTRAL PARK**
⑦ **CLARK COUNTY COLLEGE**

Exit 1D

This exit provides access to downtown Vancouver and the Port of Vancouver. It is closely tied to Exits 1B and 1C via Main St., Broadway, and Fort Vancouver Way. See Exits 1B and 1C for additional services that you can reach easily from this exit.

Key Features: Downtown Vancouver.

Towing: Vancouver Towing 696-0441; Chappelle's Towing 696-1710

Northbound:

Southbound:

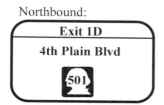

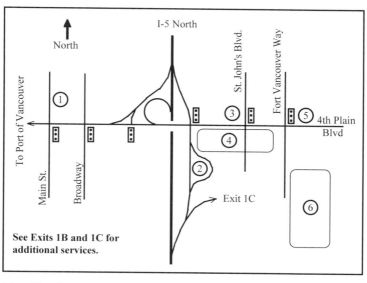

Fast Food

① DAIRY QUEEN (phone)
⑤ BURGERVILLE

③ VANCOUVER VETERINARY HOSPITAL

Other

② INFORMATION CENTER
 • Maps & tourist information
 • Wheelchair-accessible restrooms
 • Pet area
 • Phone

④ VA MEDICAL CENTER

⑥ VANCOUVER CENTRAL PARK

Everybody's coming to Washington: The Columbia River Bridge between Portland, Oregon, and Vancouver, Washington.

Exit 2

This exit provides emergency medical services, a park in which to unwind, and 24-hour gas and food. Additional services are available at Exit 1D, which can be reached from this exit by going South on Main Street. See Exit 1D for additional details.

Key Features: 24-hour gas, food, and medical services.

Towing: Vancouver Towing 696-0441; Chappelle's Towing 696-1710

Northbound:

Exit 2		
39th St. **Hospital**	**500**	**East** **Orchards**

Southbound:

Exit 2
39th St.

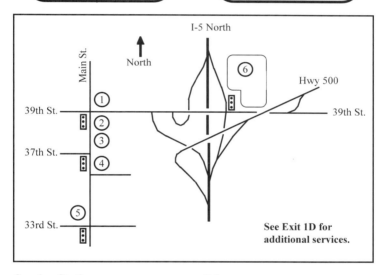

Service Stations

① **MAIN STREET ASTRO** 6:30am- 8pm Mon-Fri. 7:30am-6pm Sat-Sun. Full-serve, cash & credit cards, phone, propane, restrooms. Mechanic available 8am-4pm, Mon-Fri.

② **ARCO AM/PM**   24 Hrs. Self-serve, mini-mart, cash & cash-machine cards, phone, restrooms.

Other

③ **SAFEWAY** (24 Hrs.)

④ **FIRE STATION**

⑤ **VANCOUVER MEMORIAL HOSPITAL**

⑥ **LEVERICH PARK**
 • 5am-10pm, 7 days
 • Play area, restrooms
 • Covered picnic areas
 • Baseball field

Exit 3

This exit is at the North end of Vancouver and connects to Exit 2 via 39th Street and Exit 4 via Hwy. 99 or Hazel Dell Road (residential). Southbound, the easiest way to use the services at this exit is to get off at Exit 4 and drive South on Hwy. 99, getting back on I-5 at Exit 3. Northbound is just the reverse. You're bound to find what you need at this exit.

Key Features: 24-hour gas, food, and lodging.

Towing: Triple J Towing 254-8552 or 693-5089
Chappelle's Towing 696-1710

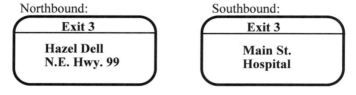

Northbound:

Exit 3
Hazel Dell **N.E. Hwy. 99**

Southbound:

Exit 3
Main St. **Hospital**

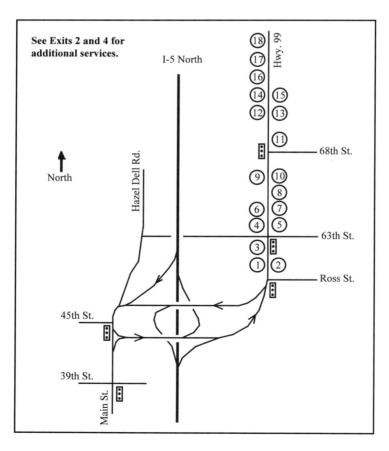

Exit 3 *continued*

Service Stations

③ **7-11 (CITGO)**   24 Hrs.
Self-serve, cash & credit cards,
phone, large mini-mart, no
restrooms.

⑪ **TEXACO**   24 Hrs.
Self-serve, cash & credit cards,
diesel, drive-thru car wash with
do-it-yourself truck or RV
washing, RV pump-out, no
restrooms.

Restaurants

⑨ **TEE-DEE'S PIE HOUSE** $$
6am-midnight, 7 days. Full-
service restaurant with counter
and take-out service, featuring
an American menu with pies to
go. Cash & credit cards.

⑮ **REUNION** $$
11am-9pm Mon-Thur, 11am-
10pm Fri, 5pm-10pm Sat, 4pm-
9pm Sun. Full-service restaurant
featuring an American menu,
specializing in seafood and
steak. Cash & credit cards &
checks. Full bar.

Fast Food

② **A&W HAMBURGERS**

⑥ **SKIPPER'S**

⑦ **PIZZA HUT**

⑧ **TACO TIME**

⑩ **SUBWAY**

⑫ **SMOKEY'S PIZZA**

⑭ **BASKIN-ROBBINS**

⑯ **TACO BELL** (24 Hrs.)

⑰ **McDONALD'S**

⑱ **STEAKBURGER**

Lodging

⑬ **NENDEL'S SUITES** ☺☺☺ $$$
1-800-547-0106 Non-smoking
rooms available. All rooms
have kitchenettes. Cash &
credit cards & checks. Phones,
cable TV. Pets OK with fee.
Discounts & weekly rates
available. Guest laundry, VCR
movie & machine rental, ceiling
fans in rooms (no air condition-
ing). Seasonal outdoor pool
with a year-round hot tub.
Continental breakfast served in
the lobby.

Other

① **MIDAS MUFFLER**
④ **OIL CAN HENRY'S**
    (oil changes)
⑤ **PLAZA 99**
    • Figaro's Pizza
    • Ragamuffin's Deli
    • phone
    • Wonder Bakery Thrift Shop
⑱ **GOLF-O-RAMA**
Miniature golf behind the
Steakburger restaurant. Great
place to give the kids a break
from driving.

Exit 4

This exit, just North of Vancouver, connects to Exit 3 via Hwy 99 or Hazel Dell Road (residential). Southbound, the easiest way to use the services at this exit is to drive South on Hwy 99, getting back on the freeway at Exit 3. Northbound is just the reverse. If you can't find what you need at this exit, you didn't look hard enough!

Key Features: 24-hour gas, food, and lodging.

Towing:
Speed's Towing 696-5678
Chappelle's Towing 696-1710

> **Exit 4**
>
> **N.E. 78 St.**

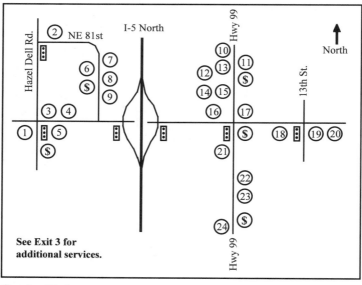

See Exit 3 for additional services.

Service Stations

① **SHELL** 6am-11pm, 7 days. Self- & full-serve, cash & credit cards, phone, restrooms, diesel, propane. Mechanic on duty 6am-5pm Mon-Sat.

③ **ARCO** 24 Hrs. Self-serve, mini-mart, cash & cash-machine cards, phone, no restrooms.

④ **TEXACO** 24 Hrs. Self-serve, mini-mart, cash & credit cards, restrooms, diesel. Drive-thru car wash.

⑩ **HAZEL DELL CAR WASH** (BP) 8am-7pm, Mon-Sat, 8am-6pm Sun. Self- & mini-serve, cash & credit cards & checks, phone, restrooms. Car wash with hand-washing & auto detailing available.

⑰ **UNOCAL 76** 24 Hrs. Self-serve, cash & credit cards, phone, no restrooms.

㉔ **CHEVRON** 24 Hrs. Self- & full-serve, large mini-mart, cash & credit cards, phone, restrooms, propane, ice. Mechanic services.

Exit 4 *continued*

Restaurants

⑪ **CHOI'S DYNASTY** $$
11:30am-10pm Mon-Thur,
11:30am-11pm Fri, noon-11pm
Sat, noon-10pm Sun. Full-
service restaurant with take-out
available. Chinese menu. Full
bar. Cash & credit cards.

⑬ **SAKURA** $$
Lunch: 11:30am-2pm Mon-Fri,
Dinner: 5pm-9:30pm Mon-Thur,
5pm-10pm Fri-Sat. Full-service
restaurant featuring a Japanese
menu specializing in sushi.
Cash & credit cards. Full bar.

⑭ **MAMA'S BAKE SHOP** $$
6am-9pm Sun-Thur, 6am-10pm
Fri-Sat. Full-service restaurant
with take-out available,
featuring an American menu
specializing in desserts,
especially take-out pies, cakes,
& cookies. Cash & credit cards.
Full bar. If you're in the mood
for something sweet, try this!

⑳ **DRAGON KING** $$
11:30am-11pm Mon-Thur,
11:30am-12am Fri-Sat, 11:30-
10pm Sun. Full-service
restaurant with take-out
available & a buffet lunch.
Chinese menu. Full bar. Cash &
credit cards. Limited wheelchair access.

㉑ **TOTEM POLE** $$
7am-11pm, 7 days. Full-service
restaurant with counter service
& take-out available. American
menu specializing in seafood &
"TeePee's chicken." Beer &
wine. Cash & credit cards.

㉒ **THE NEW HONG KONG** $$
11am-2am Mon-Sat, 12am-
12pm Sun. Full-service
restaurant. Chinese & American
menu. Full bar. Cash & credit
cards.

Fast Food

⑥ **WENDY'S**
⑦ **PIETRO'S PIZZA**
⑨ **DENNY'S**
⑮ **ROUND TABLE PIZZA**
⑯ **BURGERVILLE**
⑱ **KENTUCKY FRIED CHICKEN**
⑲ **LITTLE CAESAR'S PIZZA**
㉓ **BURGER KING**

Lodging

⑧ **BEST WESTERN FERRYMAN'S
INN** ☺☺ $$$ (206) 574-2151
Non-smoking and handicapped
rooms available, some with
kitchenettes. Cash & credit
cards & checks. Phones, cable
TV. Pets OK with fee. Discounts
& weekly rates available.
Secured guest laundry. Seasonal
outdoor pool. Continental
breakfast served in the lobby.
Very friendly. *Attached
restaurant:* Yansing. Chinese
menu. Full bar, 576-1918,
11am-11pm Sun-Thur, 11am-
12am Fri-Sat. Discount for
guests.

Other

② **SAFEWAY** (24 Hrs.)
⑤ **78TH STREET MARKETPLACE**
   • Hall's Pharmacy
   • Village Optical
   • Hallmark, Post Office
   • Phone

Exit 7

This exit (Southbound) provides a bypass around downtown Portland, reconnecting with I-5 South of the city. Both motels at this exit are bargains for the traveller, with breakfast included in the price of the room.

Key Features: 24-hour gas, food, and lodging at a quiet exit.

Towing:
Orchard's Towing 892-3564
Chappelle's Towing 696-1710

Southbound:

> **NE 134th St.**
> **Portland Airport**
> **Use I-205**

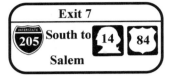

Northbound:

> **Exit 7**
>
> **N.E. 134th St.**

Southbound on I-205:

> **Exit 36**
>
> **NE 134th**
> **Hazel Dell**

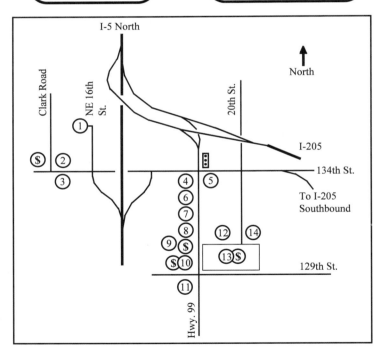

Service Stations

③ **EXPRESS WAY FOOD STORE**
6am-11pm, Mon-Sat, 7am-10pm Sun. Self-serve, large mini-mart, cash only, phone, no restrooms.

⑥ **UNOCAL 76**   24 Hrs.
Self- & full-serve, cash & credit cards, phone, restrooms, propane. Diesel technician (mechanic) on duty 7 days a week.

Exit 7 *continued*

⑩ **7-11 (CITGO)**   24 Hrs.
Self-serve, large mini-mart,
cash & credit cards & checks,
no restrooms. Cash machine in
store.

⑫ **TRAIL MART**   6:30am-12am,
7 days. Self-serve, large mini-
mart, cash & credit cards &
checks, phone, no restrooms.

Restaurants

⑨ **STAGE COACH INN** $$
6:30am-10pm Mon-Sat, 8am-
8pm Sun. Full-service restau-
rant with take-out available,
featuring an American menu.
Full bar. Cash & credit cards.
Live entertainment, dancing on
Fri & Sat. Good food at
reasonable prices, salad bar, &
a quiet atmosphere.

Fast Food

④ **BURGER KING**
⑤ **BURGERVILLE**
⑧ **TACO BELL**
⑫ **ROUND TABLE PIZZA**

Lodging

⑦ **SHILO INN**   ☺☺☺ $$$
1-800-222-2244 Non-smoking
rooms available, some with
kitchenettes. Cash & credit
cards. Discounts available.
Phones, cable TV. Pets OK
with fee. Guest laundry. Indoor
heated pool with steam room &
sauna. Continental breakfast
served in the lobby. Popcorn &
coffee available in lobby all
night.

⑭ **COMFORT INN** ☺☺☺ $$$
1-800-221-2222 Non-smoking
& handicapped rooms available.
Most rooms have kitchenettes.
Cash & credit cards. Discounts
available, weekly rates available
in Winter. Phones, guest
laundry, cable TV. Pets OK (no
fee). Indoor heated pool with
exercise area & spa. Continental
breakfast in comfortable lobby.

Other

① **MOUNTAIN VIEW**
   VETERINARY HOSPITAL
② **FIRE STATION**
⑪ **99 MOBILE LODGE RV PARK**
   • (206) 573-0351
   • Spaces available daily,
     weekly, monthly, &
     permanently.
⑬ **SALMON CREEK PLAZA**
   • Food Pavilion (24 Hrs.)
   • Round Table Pizza
   • Western Union
   • Hi-School Pharmacy
   • True-Value Hardware
   • Coin-Op Laundromat
     7am-10pm, 7 days.
   • phone

I-205   39+ miles

Exit 9

Take this exit for the Clark County Fairgrounds or gas and food.

Key Features: Clark County Fairgrounds

Towing: Chappelle's Towing 696-1710, Speed's Towing 696-3678

Northbound:

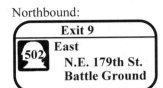

Southbound:

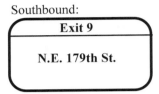

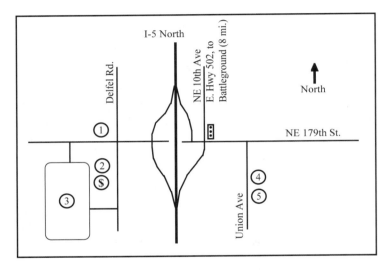

Service Stations

① **SHELL**   6am-9pm 7 days. Self-serve, mini-mart, diesel, cash & credit cards, phone, restrooms.

Restaurants

② **KRACKLES GRILL** $$ 7am-11pm 7 days. Full-service restaurant with take-out available, featuring an American menu & pizza. Beer & wine. Cash & credit cards.

④ **JOLLIE'S** $$ 24 Hrs. Full-service restaurant with counter service, featuring an American menu. Full bar. Cash & credit cards & checks. Ample truck parking available.

Other

③ **CLARK COUNTY FAIRGROUND**

⑤ **U-NEEK RV CENTER**
- 8am-6pm Mon-Fri, 9am-5pm Sat, 11am-5pm Sun
- Propane available Mon-Sat

Gee Creek Rest Area

Northbound: At mile-marker 11, the Gee Creek Rest Area features:

- RV pump-out
- Vending machines
- Free coffee
- Continuous weather broadcasts
- Visitor information booth

Southbound: At mile-marker 13:

- RV pumpout
- Free coffee

Truck Weigh Station

Northbound: At mile-marker 15, the truck weigh station provides a safe place to stop, as well as a phone and a mailbox.

Rest areas in Washington are exceptionally nice. Rest rooms are clean and well-maintained. Most rest areas provide free coffee. (Coffee and cookies are supplied by volunteers from various charitable organizations. They welcome donations, but donations aren't necessary.) Most rest areas also provide visitor information, vending machines, and covered picnic areas. There is always a pleasantly landscaped place to walk your dog. There is often an RV pump-out provided for people travelling in RVs, as well.

Exit 14

This exit has easy on-and-off access, 24-hour gas and diesel, good food, and camping.

Key Features: 24-hour fuel, including diesel, and an excellent restaurant.

Towing:
Orchards Towing 892-3564

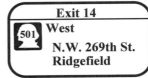

Exit 14

501 **West**
N.W. 269th St.
Ridgefield

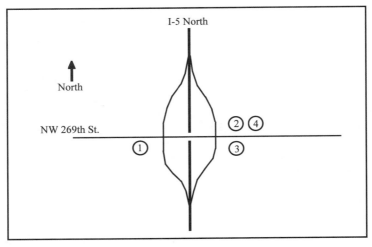

Service Stations

① BP 24 Hrs.
Self-serve, mini-mart, diesel, restrooms, phone, cash & credit cards.

② ARCO AM/PM 24 Hrs.
Self-serve, mini-mart, restrooms, phone, cash & credit cards.

③ CIRCLE K 24 Hrs.
Self-serve, large mini-mart, restroom, phone, cash & credit cards & checks, ice, and bait.

Restaurants

④ COUNTRY JUNCTION $$
6 am - 10 pm, 7 days. Full service with take-out available. Cash & credit cards. American menu with some Mexican & Italian dishes, specializing in fresh turkey. Beer & wine. Rustic atmosphere with a small gift shop, phones. Food is outstanding & worth a special stop.

Exit 16

This exit has easy on-and-off access with 24-hour gas and diesel.
Paradise Park is nearby for campers.

Key Features: 24-hour fuel
and food, Paradise Park.

Towing:
Mitch's Towing 225-6372

```
┌─────────────────────────────┐
│          Exit 16            │
├─────────────────────────────┤
│      N.W. 319th St.         │
│      La Center              │
└─────────────────────────────┘
```

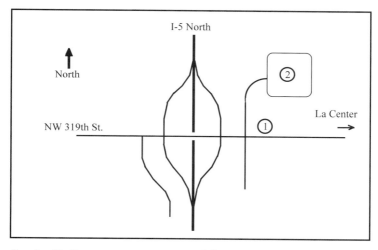

Service Stations

① **Texaco**   24 Hrs.
Self-serve, deli & large mini-mart
with sit-down dining, diesel,
restrooms, phone, cash & credit
cards & checks, propane, &
kerosene.

Other

② **Paradise Park**   Open all
year for camping. 0.7 miles from
the exit. (Only open weekends in
Winter.)

Exit 21 98674

This exit leads to Mt. St. Helens National Park, fishing and picnicking at Horseshoe Lake Park, and the Hulda Klager Lilac Gardens. A Tourist Information Center is also at this exit.

Key Features: Mt. St. Helens National Park, recreational areas, 24-hour gas, food, and lodging, Hulda Klager Lilac Gardens

Towing: Mitch's Towing 225-6372; Jack's Towing 225-8765

Northbound:

Exit 21
503 East Woodland Cougar   **Mt. St. Helens**

Southbound:

Exit 21
503 East Woodland Cougar

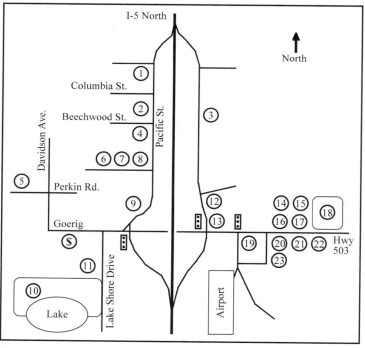

Safeway 1725 Pacific Ave

Service Stations

② **SHELL**   5am-10pm, 7 days. Self- & full-serve, diesel, phone, restrooms, cash & credit cards, propane & kerosene. Mechanic available for minor repairs.

⑧ **MINIT MART**   5am-11pm Mon-Thur, 5am-11:30pm Fri-Sat, 6am-11pm Sun. Self-serve, large mini-mart, no restrooms, phone, limited wheelchair access.

⑨ **TEXACO**   7am-7pm Mon-Fri, 8am-5pm Sat, 9am-4pm Sun. Self-serve, restrooms, cash & credit cards. Mechanic available.

⑬ **CHEVRON**   24 Hrs. Self-serve, small mini-mart, phone, restrooms, cash & credit cards.

Exit 21 *continued*

⑯ SHELL   6am-10pm, Mon-Sat, 8am-10pm Sun. Self- & full-serve, restrooms, phone, cash & credit cards, propane, diesel, & ice. Mechanic available for minor repairs, towing, & emergency road service. Days: 225-8261, evenings: 225-7957.

⑲ ARCO AM/PM   24 Hrs. Self-serve, mini-mart, restrooms, phone, cash & cash-machine cards.

㉒ TEXACO 5-midnight 7 days. Self-serve, large mini-mart, restrooms, phone, cash & credit cards. Fresh doughnuts daily, ice, & 16 flavors of ice cream.

Restaurants

⑫ OAK TREE $$ 7am-10pm, Sun-Thur, 7am-12am Fri-Sat. Full service with take-out available, cash & credit cards. American menu with great bakery, full bar, and a large gift shop. You should see the cinnamon rolls!

Fast Food

① WHIMPY'S BURGERS
⑥ LUMBERJACK PIZZA
⑰ DAIRY QUEEN
㉑ BURGERVILLE
㉓ SUBWAY
㉓ EL TACO GRANDE

Lodging

③ WOODLANDER INN ☺☺☺ $$ 1-800-444-9667, local: 225-6548 Non-smoking & handicapped rooms available, adding kitchenettes. Cash & credit cards. Discounts available, including weekly rates. Phones, cable TV. Pets OK with fee. Shuttle service, indoor pool and spa. Coffee in lobby. Lovely decor in rooms.

④ HANSEN'S MOTEL $$ Reviewers did not see rooms. (206) 225-7018 Cash & credit cards. Phones, cable TV. Pets OK with fee. Covered parking, queen-size beds. All showers, no tubs. No wheelchair access.

⑦ SCANDIA MOTEL ☺☺ $$ (206) 225-8006 or 225-7860 Non-smoking rooms available, some kitchenettes. Cash & credit cards & checks. AAA discount, weekly rates. Phones, cable TV, spa. Pets OK with fee. Guest laundry, some two-bedroom suites, in-room coffee makers.

⑪ LAKESIDE MOTEL ☺☺ $$ (206) 225-8240 Non-smoking & handicapped rooms available. Cash & credit cards. Phones, cable TV. Pets OK (no fee). Weekly rates available. Seven suites available. On lake, with fishing, city park, picnic area, & boat ramp nearby. Best bet at this exit for families needing more than one bedroom.

⑳ LEWIS RIVER INN ☺☺☺ $$ 1-800-543-4344, local: 225-6257 Non-smoking & handicapped rooms available. Cash & credit cards. Phones, cable TV. Pets OK with fee. Discounts available, including weekly rates. Ten units overlook the river. Coffee in very comfortable lobby.

Other

⑤ HULDA KLAGER LILAC GARDENS National Historic Site featuring an arboretum with many exotic plants. (206) 225-8996 for information. House tours March-June

⑩ HORSESHOE LAKE PARK Fishing, boat ramp, picnicking, & a children's play area.

⑭ COIN-OP CAR WASH
⑮ TOURIST INFO. CENTER
⑱ WOODLAND MALL
   • Thriftway, phone
   • Other Stores

Exit 22

There are no services at this exit, but it's a good place to stop and stretch, if you need to.

Key Features: No services.

> **Exit 22**
>
> **Dike Access Road**

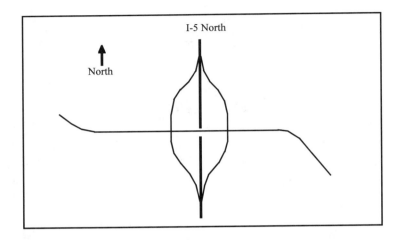

The next three exits lead to the town of Kalama. Kalama is a center for the timber industry and very picturesque, perched on a hillside on the East side of I-5. There are many interesting antique stores downtown. Kalama is a great place to stop for lunch (great sandwiches at the Columbia Inn Restaurant), followed by a stroll through the antique stores.

Exit 27

This exit leads to the Port of Kalama.

Key Features: Port of Kalama, 24-hour gas, diesel, and food.

Exit 27

**Todd Road
Port of Kalama**

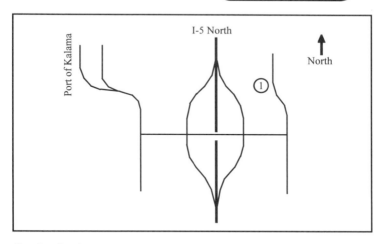

Service Stations

① **TEXACO**   24 Hrs.
Self-serve, diesel, phone, propane, restrooms, cash & credit cards. Cafe in station with inside service or food to go.

Port of Kalama, Exit 27

Exit 30

This exit leads to downtown Kalama, with its numerous antique shops containing lots of interesting items, 24-hour food, gas, and lodging.

Key Features: Downtown Kalama, antique shops

Towing:
J&B Towing 673-4030

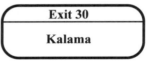

Exit 30

Kalama

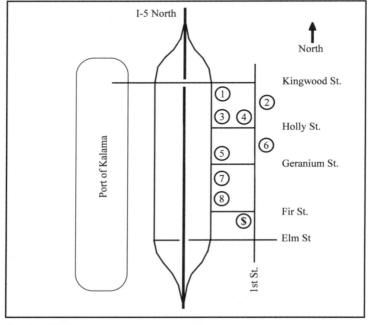

I-5 North

North

Kingwood St.

Holly St.

Geranium St.

Fir St.

Elm St

Port of Kalama

1st St.

Service Stations

⑥ **BP**   24 Hrs.
Self-serve, large mini-mart, phone, restrooms, cash & credit cards.

Restaurants

① **COLUMBIA INN** $$
6am-12am, 7 days. Full & counter service with take-out available. Cash & credit cards. American menu. Full bar. Small gift shop. Wonderful hamburgers, biscuits, pies!

⑦ **KALAMA CAFE** $$
6am-10pm, Sun-Thur, open 24 hrs. Fri-Sat. Full & counter service with take-out available. Cash & credit cards. American menu, specializing in sandwiches. Full bar.

Fast Food

④ **ONCE UPON A TEA TIME DELI**

⑧ **BURGER BAR**

Lodging

③ **COLUMBIA INN MOTEL** ☺ $$
(206) 673-2855 Non-smoking rooms available. Some rooms have kitchenettes. Cash & credit cards. Discounts available, including weekly rates. Phones, cable TV. Pets OK.

Other

① **GREYHOUND BUS STOP**
    (at restaurant)

② **COIN-OP LAUNDRY**

⑤ **FIRE DEPARTMENT**

Exit 32

This exit features an RV park with tourist info and a boat ramp.

Key Features: RV park.

Towing:
J&B Towing 673-4030

Exit 32

Kalama River
Road

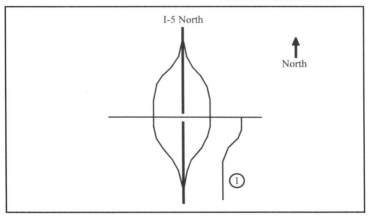

Other

① **CAMP KALAMA CAMPGROUND AND RV PARK** (206) 673-2456 Open all year, with a store that's open 10am-6pm Mon-Sat. Phone, showers, laundry, boat ramp, propane, RV pump-out, & shuttle service to Kalama. Dave's Mobile RV Service, 24 Hrs., 737-4775 or 694-8796.

Downtown Kalama, Exit 30

Truck melted during the eruption of Mt. St. Helens, Exit 21.

Exit 36

This exit is the intersection of Interstate 5 with Washington State Highway 432. There are no services immediately adjacent to this exit.

Key Features: No services

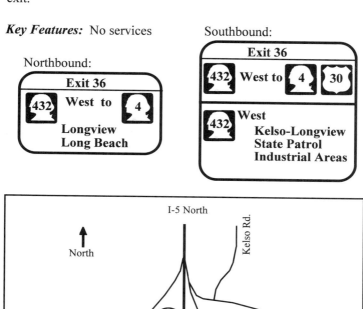

Northbound:

Exit 36

432 West to **4**

Longview
Long Beach

Southbound:

Exit 36

432 West to **4** **30**

432 West
Kelso-Longview
State Patrol
Industrial Areas

I-5 North

North

Kelso Rd.

Hwy 432

Old Hwy 99, to
Rose Valley and
Carrolls

Exit 39

This exit features the Three Rivers Mall and numerous restaurants and motels. If you just need a place to get out and walk around for awhile, try the river walk in Tam-O-Shanter Park.

Key Features: Three Rivers Mall, Mt. St. Helens exhibit at the Volcano information center, Tam-O-Shanter Park

Towing: Carl's Towing 423-4460,
Jacobsen Chevron & Towing 423-3870

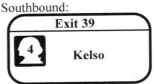

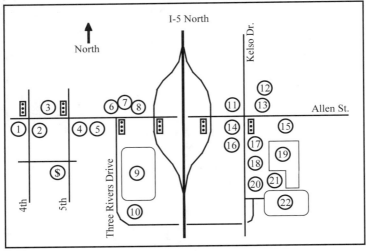

Service Stations

② **CHEVRON**   7am-10pm
7days. Self- & partial-serve, propane, phone, restrooms, cash & credit cards. Mechanic: 8am-4:30pm Mon-Fri, 9am-3pm Sat.

④ **TEXACO**   5am-12am
Sun-Thurs, 5am-2am Fri-Sat. Self-serve, large mini-mart, phone, restrooms, cash & credit cards.

⑭ **SHELL**   24 Hrs.
Self-serve, large mini-mart with 28 flavors of ice cream, RV pump-out, phone, restrooms with handicapped access, ice, cash & credit cards.

⑮ **ARCO AM/PM**   24 Hrs.
Self-serve, mini-mart, phone, restrooms, cash & cash-machine cards.

Restaurants

⑬ **HILANDER** $$
6:30am-11pm Sun-Thurs, 6:30am-12am Fri-Sat. Full & counter service. Cash & credit cards. American menu. Full bar. Attached bowling alley & Mt. St. Helens Gift Shop.

Exit 39 *continued* — *Cowlitz County Historical Museum*

Fast Food

- ⑥ TACO BELL
- ⑧ BURGER KING
- ⑯ SHARI'S
- ⑰ DENNY'S
- ⑱ McDONALD'S

Lodging

⑩ COMFORT INN ☺☺☺ $$$
(206) 425-4600 Non-smoking &
handicapped rooms available.
Some rooms with kitchenettes,
refrigerators, some suites with
whirlpools. Cash & credit cards
& checks. Discounts available.
Phones, cable TV, indoor pool
& spa. No pets. Continental
breakfast served in lobby. VCR
& tape rental, fax, copy service
available, meeting rooms.

⑫ MOTEL 6 ☺ $$
(206) 425-3229 Non-smoking
rooms available. Cash & credit
cards & checks (with 14-day
advance reservations only).
Phones, TV, outdoor pool. Pets
OK (no fee).

⑳ RED LION INN Reviewers
not permitted to see rooms.
(206) 425-4002 Cash & credit
cards & checks. Phones, cable
TV, outdoor pool. Room
service, laundry, valet, shuttle to
Kelso Airport & Portland
International Airport. Meeting
rooms. Three family suites.
Coffee shop ($$). Restaurant
open for dinner only ($$$), full
bar, American menu.

㉑ SUPER 8 MOTEL $$
Under construction when reviewed.
1-800-800-8000 Non-smoking &
handicapped rooms available,
some suites. Cash & credit cards.
Checks & discounts with VIP
card. Phones, cable TV, outdoor
pool, elevators. Pets OK with fee.

Other

① POLICE STATION

③ COWLITZ COUNTY
   HISTORICAL MUSEUM

⑤ RIVERSIDE ANIMAL HOSPITAL

⑦ MINIT-LUBE

⑨ THREE-RIVERS MALL
   - Top Foods (24 Hrs.)
   - JC Penney
   - Emporium
   - Sears (with Auto Center)
   - Bon Marche
   - Food Court
   - Target
   - Cinemas
   - Izzy's Pizza
   - Many smaller shops

⑪ KELSO CHAMBER OF
   COMMERCE, INFORMATION
   CENTER, AND VOLCANO
   INFORMATION
   - Winter: 9am-5pm Wed-Sun
   - Summer: 9am-5pm 7 days
   - Phone
   - Wonderful Mt. St. Helens
     exhibit. Don't miss it!

⑲ RIVERWAY PLAZA
   - Safeway (6am-12am)
   - Little Caesar's
   - Phone
   - Payless Drug

㉒ TAM-O-SHANTER PARK
   - River walk
   - Sports fields
   - Covered picnic area
   - Restrooms
   - Phone
   - Children's play area

Exit 40

This exit leads to downtown Kelso.

Key Features: Kelso, emergency auto service.

Towing: Pacific Auto Store Towing 425-4736

Northbound:

> **Exit 40**
>
> **N. Kelso Ave**

Southbound:

> **Exit 40**
>
> **South to** 【**4**】
>
> **Kelso-Longview**
> **Long Beach**

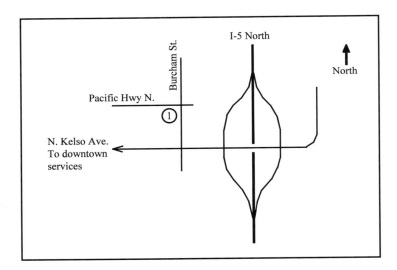

Service Stations

① **PACIFIC AUTO STORE** 7am-7pm Mon-Fri, 8am-6pm Sat, closed Sun. Self-serve, auto parts store, phone, cash & credit cards. Towing & emergency roadside service 24 Hrs.: 425-4736. Mechanic on duty 8:30am-5:30pm Mon-Fri.

Exit 42

No services at this exit: good place to change drivers or turn around.

Key Features: No services.

Northbound:

Exit 42
Ostrander Rd. **Pleasant Hill Rd.**

Southbound:

Exit 42
Ostrander **Road**

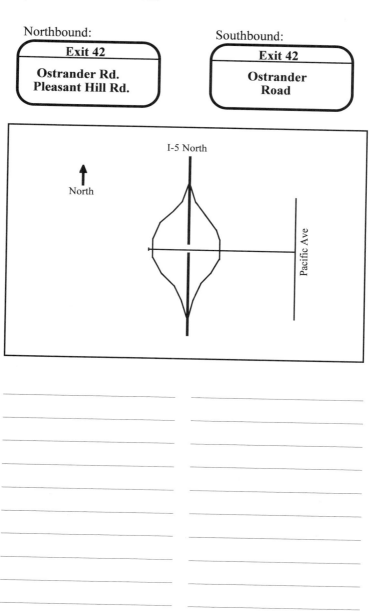

Exit 46

No services at this exit except for an RV park.
Key Features: Cedars RV Park.

Towing: Mitch's Towing 225-6372

Northbound

Exit 46
Headquarters Rd.

Southbound

Exit 46
Headquarters Rd. **Pleasant Hill Rd.**

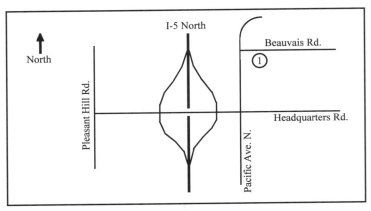

Other

① **CEDARS RV PARK** .5 mi
from exit, on Beauvais Road.

Below: Countryside at this exit.

Exit 48

No services at this exit, but there's a nice riverside park for taking a break or having a picnic.

Key Features: No services

Towing: J&B Towing 274-9816; Mitch's Towing 225-6372

Northbound:

> **Exit 48**
>
> **5** **Business Loop**
>
> **Castle Rock**

Southbound:

> **Exit 48**
>
> **Huntington Avenue**

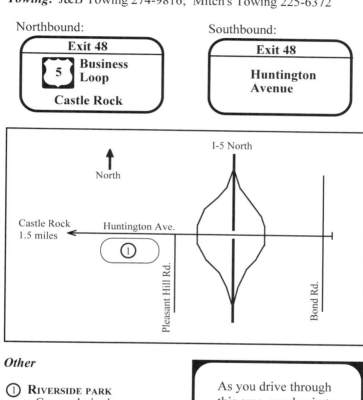

Other

① **RIVERSIDE PARK**
  • Covered picnic area
  • River view

As you drive through this area, you begin to get fabulous views of both Mt. St. Helens and Mt. Rainier to the East of I-5.

Exit 49

This exit leads to Mt. St. Helens Visitor Center (5 miles) and to Castle Rock, via WA 504. There are plenty of places to buy gas or food or to stay overnight near the exit.

Key Features: Mt. St. Helens Visitor Center, services

Towing:
J&B Towing 274-9816

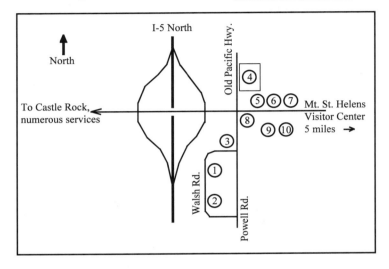

Service Stations

③ **ARCO AM/PM**   24 Hrs.
Self-serve, mini-mart, cash & cash-machine cards, phone, restrooms.

⑧ **TEXACO**   3:30am-1:00am
7days. Self-serve, large mini-mart with eating area, diesel, propane, cash & credit cards, phone, restrooms. Large truck fueling area.

Restaurants

① **PEPER'S 49ER** $$
4am-10pm 7days. Full and counter service, featuring an American menu. Cash & credit cards.

⑨ **ROSE TREE** $$
6am-10pm Sun-Thurs, 6am-11pm Fri-Sat. Full and counter service, featuring an American menu & salad bar. Cash & credit cards & checks. Full bar. Large gift shop. Beautiful stained glass.

Lodging

② **7 WEST MOTEL**   ☺ $$
(206) 274-7526 Non-smoking rooms available. One room with kitchenette, two with refrigerators. Cash & credit cards & checks. Weekly rates available. Some phones, cable TV. Pets OK with fee. Picnic area, coffee in lobby, VCR & tape rental, ice, gift shop. Truck parking available.

Exit 49 *continued*

⑦ **TIMBERLAND MOTEL** $$
Reviewers unable to see rooms.
Non-smoking rooms available,
most with refrigerators. Cash &
credit cards. Phones, cable TV,
coffee in rooms.

⑩ **MT ST HELENS MOTEL**
    ☺☺ $$ (206) 274-7721
Non-smoking & handicapped
rooms available. Some rooms
have refrigerators. Cash & credit
cards. Phones, cable TV. Pets
OK with fee. Guest laundry with
free soap. Coffee & snacks
available in lobby. Basketball
court, jogging trail. Conference
room.

Other

④ **MALL**
- Papa Pete's Pizza Parlor
- Taco Bandito

⑤ **MT. ST. HELEN'S CINEDOME
THEATER**

⑥ **COIN-OP LAUNDRY**

Exit 52

This exit features an RV park with a small store.

Key Features: RV park and a small store.

Towing: J&B Towing 274-9816

Northbound:

> ### Exit 52
> **Barnes Drive**
> **Toutle Park Rd.**

Southbound:

> ### Exit 52
> **Toutle Park**
> **Rd.**

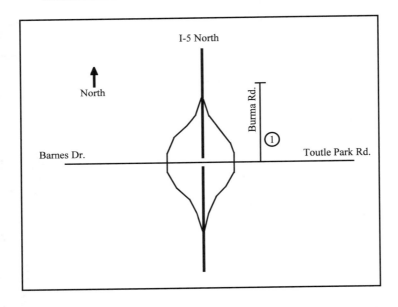

Other

① **MERMAC STORE & RV PARK**
Mini-mart, propane, phone,
restrooms (for park occupants
only), picnic area, hookups, ice.
"Woodsy" setting.

Rest Area

Northbound: At mile-marker 54, the Toutle River Rest Area features:

- Free coffee
- phones

Southbound: At mile-marker 55, the Toutle River Rest Area features:

- Free coffee
- phones

Truck Weigh Station

Southbound: At mile-marker 44, the truck weigh station provides a safe place to stop and a phone.

Most rest areas have beautiful places for picnics & walks.

Exit 57

This exit features services tailored to the long-haul trucker. Gas for cars and RVs is available at the truck stop, along with a restaurant. There is also an RV park at this exit.

Key Features: Food, gas, truck services

Towing: J&B Towing 274-9816

Northbound:

Exit 57
Jackson Hwy.

Southbound:

Exit 57
Jackson Hwy. Barnes Drive

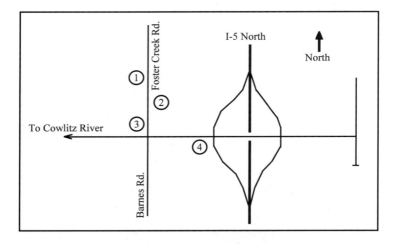

Service Stations

③ **TEXACO TRUCK STOP** 24 Hrs. Self-serve, mini-mart, cash & credit cards & cash machine cards, diesel, propane, phone, restrooms. Cafe with full service and counter service. Truck mechanic on duty 8am-10pm Mon-Fri. Rooms for truckers.

Other

① **RV PARK**
  • (206) 864-4567
  • Propane
  • Laundry

② **MACK TRUCKS**
  • Truck parts and service

④ **WESTERN STAR TRUCKS**
  • Truck parts, repair, sales
  • Open 24 Hrs: 864-4477

Exit 59

This exit leads to Vader and Ryderwood via WA 506. There is food, gas, and an RV park near the exit.

Key Features: Food and gas

Towing:
Olson Bros. Garage 864-2121
Beans Towing 864-2150
B&D Auto Repair 864-2611

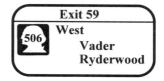

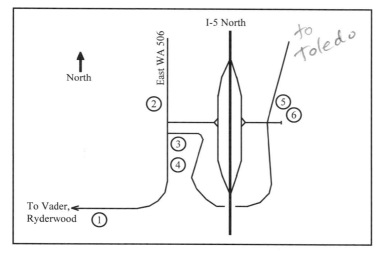

Service Stations

⑥ **BP**   6am-9pm Mon-Fri, 7am-9pm Sat-Sun. (Open until 10pm in Summer) Self-serve, cash & credit cards, phone, restrooms, diesel.

Restaurants

② **Country House Cafe** $$ 7am-9pm, 7 days. A full-service restaurant with counter, featuring an American menu. Full bar Tues-Sat. Cash & credit cards & in-State checks. Gift shop.

Fast Food

④ **Drive-In Burgers**
⑤ **Mrs. Beesley's**

Other

① **River Oaks RV Park**
  • Restrooms
  • Hookups
  • Covered picnic area
  • River access with boat ramp
  • Phone
  • Laundry

③ **B&D Auto Repair** 8am-6pm Mon-Sat, call other times. Phone: 864-2611. 24-Hour towing and road service.

Exit 60

There are no services at this exit.

Key Features: No services

Towing:
Beans Towing 864-2150

Exit 60

Toledo

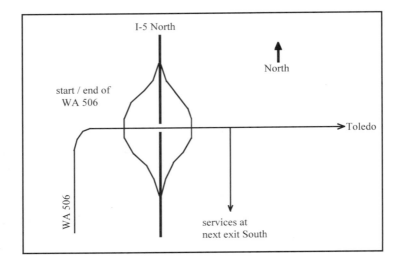

Abandoned gas station, Exit 162.

Exit 63

This exit provides access to Winlock, via WA 505. Gas and food are available one mile West of the exit.

Key Features: Gas

Towing:
Grant's Towing 748-4118

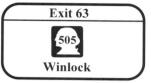

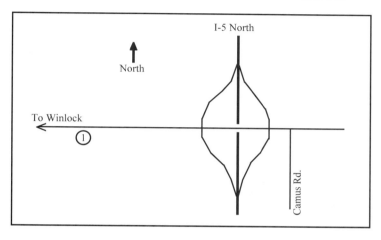

Service Stations

① **Exxon**   5am-11pm
7 days. Self-serve, large mini-mart with deli and sit-down eating area, cash & credit cards, phone, restrooms with handi-capped access.

As you drive through this area, you'll see many exhibits related to the eruption of Mt. St. Helens.

Exit 68

This exit provides access to Mt. St. Helens (48 miles West), as well as Mossyrock, Morton, & Yakima via US 12. You can get gas or a bite to eat near the exit. There's a Good Sam RV Park behind the Shell station.

Key Features: Gas, food, RV park

Towing: Grant's Towing & Repair 748-4118

Northbound: Southbound:

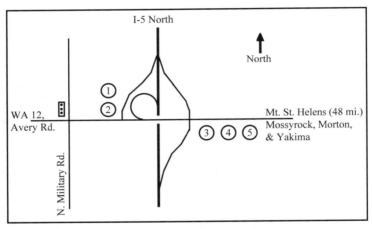

Service Stations

② **Texaco**   24 Hrs.
Self-serve, mini-mart with hot deli food & an eating area, diesel, propane, cash & credit cards, phone, restrooms.

④ **Arco am/pm**
Under construction.

⑤ **Shell**   24 Hrs.
Self-serve, mini-mart, propane, RV pump-out, cash, credit cards & checks, restrooms. Outdoor seating area. Scotty's Fruit Warehouse: large selection of animal food. Good Sam RV Park: hook-ups, restrooms.

Restaurants

① **Mustard Seed** $$
6am-7pm Mon-Fri, 6am-8pm Sat-Sun. Full-service restaurant with drive-thru, featuring an American menu. Cash & credit cards. Truck parking available.

③ **Spiffy's** $$
24 Hrs. Full & counter service, featuring an American menu with a large selection of baked goods, oversized portions of home-made pies. Gift shop. Cash & credit cards.

Exit 71

This exit provides access to Napavine and Onalaska, via WA 508. You can also get gas and food near the exit.

Key Features: Gas and food

Towing: Grant's Towing 748-4118

Northbound: Southbound:

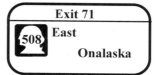

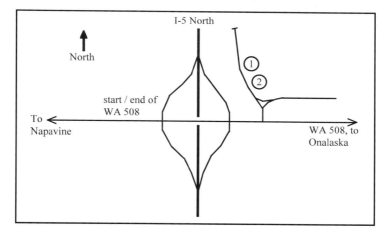

Service Stations

② **Bode's Truck Stop** 24 Hrs. (Exxon) Self-serve, mini-mart, diesel, propane, ice, cash & credit cards, phone, restrooms. 24-Hr. truck maintenance. Tire repair service: 262-3132.

Restaurants

① **Newaukum Valley Restaurant & Bakery** $$ 24 Hrs. Full-service restaurant with counter & take-out available. American menu specializing in steak, chicken, & pasta, with full bar. Cash & credit cards. Large selection of pies.

This abandoned gas station had a special flag
design built into it and painted on the bricks.

American flag on abandoned gas station at Exit 137.

Exit 72

This exit provides food, gas, and RV repair. Note that Rush Road crosses the freeway; it's on both sides.

Key Features: Food and gas

Towing: Olson Brothers' Garage 864-2121; Grant's Towing 748-4118

Northbound:

Exit 72
Rush Road **Napavine**

Southbound:

Exit 72
Rush Road

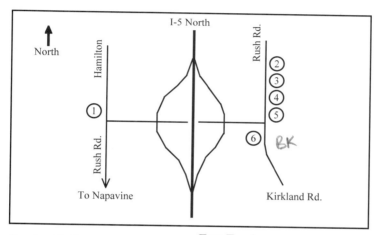

Service Stations

① **BP**   24 Hrs.
Self-serve, large mini-mart, cash & credit cards, phone, restrooms.

④ **SHELL**   24 Hrs.
Self-serve, cash & credit cards & checks, diesel & truck diesel, propane, phone, restrooms, picnic tables. Extensive truck parking.

Restaurants

⑤ **RIB EYE** $$
24 Hrs. Full & counter service. American menu, specializing in steak. Full bar. Cash & credit cards. Large Sunday brunch. Extensive truck parking.

Fast Food

③ **JBOB'S IN-&-OUT**

⑥ **MCDONALD'S**

Other

② **DAVE'S COUNTRY CANOPY & RV SALES**
• RV repair, parts, supplies
• (206) 748-9721
• 8:30am-5:30pm Mon-Fri, 8:30am-2pm Sat, closed Sun

Exit 76

This exit provides access to Chehalis city center and numerous services, as well as Stan Hedwall Park & Chehalis Recreation Park.

Key Features: Chehalis city center, parks

Towing:
Grant's Towing 748-4118

Exit 76
13th St.

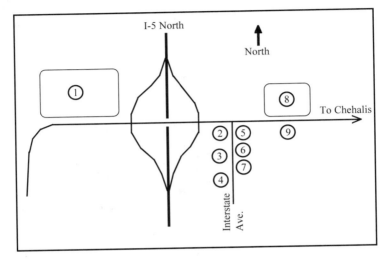

Service Stations

② **ARCO AM/PM**   24 Hrs.
Self-serve, mini-mart, cash & cash-machine cards, phone, restrooms.

Restaurants

⑥ **KIT CARSON COFFEE SHOP** $$
6am-11pm Sun-Thurs, 6am-1am Fri-Sat. Full & counter service, featuring an American menu. Full bar. Cash & credit cards & checks. You can also watch and wager on races from Yakima Meadows.

Fast Food

③ **DENNY'S**
⑦ **JACK IN THE BOX**
⑨ **PACIFIC PIZZA** (748-4400)

Lodging

④ **PONY SOLDIER MOTOR INN**
1-800-634-PONY   ☺☺ $$
Non-smoking rooms available. All rooms have refrigerators. Cash & credit cards & checks. Discounts available. Phones, cable TV. Pets OK with fee. Outdoor heated pool and hot tub. Continental breakfast served in one room reserved for that purpose. Coffee available in lobby 24 Hrs. Meetings rooms, fax, copy machine available.

⑤ **CASCADE MOTEL** ☺☺ $$
(206) 748-8608   All non-smoking rooms. Cash & credit cards. Discounts available. Phones, cable TV. No pets.

Exit 76 *continued*

Other

① STAN HEDWALL PARK
  - Large sports fields
  - Covered picnic area with grills

⑧ CHEHALIS RECREATION PARK
  - Pool
  - Covered picnic area
  - Sports fields
  - Children's play area
  - Phone

This *Pepsi* machine is in jail at Exit 59.

Exit 77

This exit provides access to downtown Chehalis, via Main Street. It also leads to Pe Ell and Raymond via WA 6.

Key Features: Downtown
Chehalis, services

Towing:
Grant's Towing 748-4118

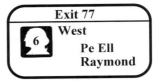

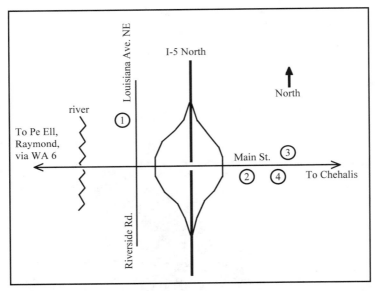

Service Stations

② **BP**   7am-7pm Mon-Fri, 8am-7pm Sat, 8:30am-5pm Sun. Partial-serve, cash & credit cards, phone, restrooms. Mechanic available for minor work, such as replacing tires & oil changes.

③ JACKPOT FOOD MART
24 Hrs. (Arco) Self-serve, cash only, phone, ice.

Fast Food

④ DAIRY BAR BURGERS

Other

① CHEHALIS RENTALS
  • (206) 748-6619
  • Propane

Exit 79

This exit provides access to food, gas, and numerous downtown services in Chehalis.

Key Features: Food and gas

Towing: Grant's Towing 748-4118; Charlie's Towing 736-4019

Northbound:

> **Exit 79**
>
> **Chamber Way**

Southbound:

> **Exit 79**
>
> **Chamber Way**
> **City Center**

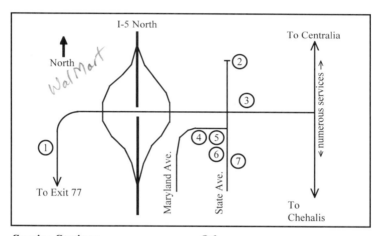

Service Stations

⑤ **TEXACO**　　5am-10pm, Mon-Fri, 6am-10pm Sat-Sun. Self-serve, large mini-mart, diesel, propane, cash & credit cards, phone, restrooms.

Restaurants

④ **PLAZA JALISCO**　　$$ 11am-9pm Mon, 11am-10pm Tues-Thurs, 11am-11pm Fri-Sat, 11am-9pm Sun. Full-service restaurant featuring a Mexican menu. Full bar. Cash & credit cards.

Other

① **STATE PATROL**

② **UHLMANN TOYOTA & RV CENTER**
 • Propane
 • 8:30am-5:30pm Mon-Fri, 9am-5pm Sat, closed Sun

③ **VISITOR INFORMATION CENTER & CHAMBER OF COMMERCE**
 • Phone

⑥ **GOODYEAR TIRES & SERVICE**
 • 8am-6pm Mon-Fri, 8am-5pm Sat, closed Sun

⑦ **CHEHALIS/CENTRALIA VETERINARY HOSPITAL**

Exit 81

This exit provides gas, food, and two very nice motels that are outstanding bargains.

Key Features: Gas, food, excellent motels

Towing: Charlie's Towing 736-4019, Grant's Towing 748-4118

Northbound:

Southbound:

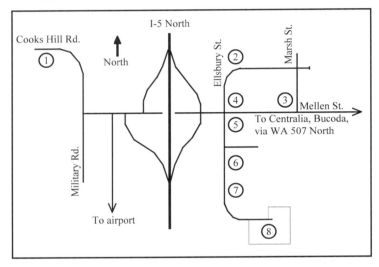

Service Stations

⑤ **Texaco** 24 Hrs. Self-serve, large mini-mart serving hot food, cash & credit cards, phone, restrooms.

⑥ **Shell** 7am-9pm, 7days. Self- & full-serve, small mini-mart, cash & credit cards & checks, phone, restrooms, propane, RV pump-out with fill-up. AAA-approved auto repair. Mechanic on duty from 8am-5pm Mon-Fri, 7am-3pm Sat-Sun.

Restaurants

④ **King Solomon** $$ 6am-10pm Sun-Thurs, 6am-11pm Fri-Sat. Full & counter service. American menu specializing in steak and chicken. Full bar. Cash & credit cards.

⑦ **Peppermill** $$ 6am-9pm, 7 days. Full & counter service. American menu specializing in mouth-watering pies. Full bar. Cash & credit cards.

③ **Winter Kitchen** Open for lunch 11am to 4pm Mon-Sat.

Exit 81 *continued*

Lodging

② **LAKE SHORE MOTEL** ☺☺☺
(206)736-9344 $$
Non-smoking rooms available,
some with refrigerators. Several
suites available. Cash & credit
cards. Discounts and weekly
rates available. Phones, cable
TV with Showtime. No pets.
Rooms just remodelled, have
in-room coffee. Motel located
overlooking a lake open for
swimming in the summer.
Rooms open onto the lake;
upstairs rooms have a balcony.
Picnic area. Terrific value.

⑧ **PEPPERTREE MOTEL & RV
     PARK**   ☺☺☺ $$
(206) 736-1124 Non-smoking
and handicapped rooms
available. Some rooms have
kitchenettes, some have
refrigerators. All rooms are at
ground-level. Cash & credit
cards & checks. Weekly rates
available. Phones, cable TV.
Pets OK with fee. Rooms have
been recently remodelled.
Another terrific value. RV park
has showers & RV pump-out.

Other

① **PROVIDENCE HOSPITAL**

Exit 82

This exit provides access to the Centralia factory outlet stores, Fort Borst Park, and lots of places to eat or spend the night.

Key Features: Factory outlet stores, Fort Borst Park

Towing: All-Ways Towing 736-6258; B&D Towing 736-0700

Northbound:

Exit 82
Harrison Ave.

Southbound:

Exit 82
Centralia

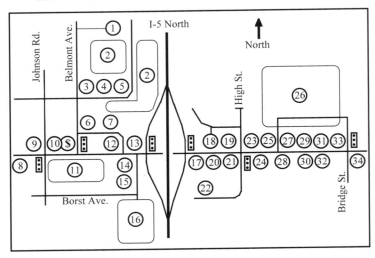

Service Stations

⑨ **TEXACO** 6am-11pm, 7 days. Self-serve, large mini-mart, cash & credit cards, phone, no restrooms.

⑬ **CHEVRON** 24 Hrs. Self- & full-serve, cash & credit cards, phone, restrooms.

⑲ **ARCO AM/PM** 24 Hrs. Self-serve, mini-mart, cash & cash machine cards, phone, restrooms.

Restaurants

⑫ **COUNTRY COUSIN** $$ 5:30am-12pm Mon-Fri, 6am-12pm Sat-Sun. Full-service restaurant featuring American menu. Full bar. Cash & credit cards & checks. Country atmosphere with large gift shop.

⑳ **CASA RAMOS** $$ 11am-10pm Mon-Thur, 11am-11pm Fri-Sat, 10am-10pm Sun. Full-service Mexican restaurant. Full bar. Cash & credit cards. Sunday brunch from 10am-2pm.

㉕ **MR. D'S** $$ 6am-9pm Sun-Thur, 6am-10pm Fri-Sat. Full-service restaurant specializing in seafood & steak. Full bar. Cash & credit cards & checks. Sunday Brunch.

Fast Food

③ **ARBY'S**

④ **ANDREE'S COFFEE HOUSE**

⑤ **MCDONALD'S**

⑥ **TACO BELL**

⑦ **DENNY'S**

Exit 82 *continued*

- ⑧ BILL & BEA'S BURGERS
- ⑩ SUBWAY
- ⑪ LITTLE CAESAR'S PIZZA
- ⑪ SUB SHOP
- ⑰ SHARI'S
- ㉓ BURGERVILLE
- ㉔ WENDY'S
- ㉗ QUICK'S BURGERS
- ㉘ BURGER KING
- ㉙ GODFATHER'S PIZZA
- ㉚ PIZZA HUT
- ㉜ CATLIN'S (24 Hrs)

Lodging

① MOTEL 6 ☺ $$
(206) 330-2057 Non-smoking &
handicapped rooms available.
Cash & credit cards & checks (14
days in advance). Phones, cable
TV, pets OK. Showers only (no
tubs), outdoor heated pool.
Convenient to shopping malls.

⑭ PARK MOTEL ☺☺ $$
(206) 736-9333 Non-smoking
rooms available. Some family
suites, & some kitchenettes. Cash
& credit cards. Discounts
available. Phones, cable TV. Pets
OK with fee. Coffee in room.
Limited handicapped access.
Very convenient to malls, right
next to the park.

⑱ FERRYMAN'S INN ☺☺☺ $$
(206) 330-2094 Non-smoking &
handicapped rooms available,
some kitchenettes. Cash & credit
cards & checks. Discounts
available. Phones, cable TV. Pets
OK with fee. Continental
breakfast, coffee & snacks in
lobby. Outdoor heated pool,
spa, complimentary visit to a
fitness center, fax, copy
machine, & guest laundry.

㉛ HUNTLEY INN ☺☺☺ $$
1-800-448-5544 or (206) 736-2875
Non-smoking & handicapped
rooms available, some refrigerators. Cash, credit cards & checks.
Discounts available; weekly rates
in Winter. Phones, cable TV. Pets
OK with fee. Continental breakfast
in lobby. Outdoor pool, 3 rooms
with spas. Fax & guest laundry.
Sea-Tac Airporter Shuttle stops
here. Adjacent to park.

㉝ RIVERSIDE MOTEL ☺ $$
(206) 736-4632 One non-smoking
room available. Weekly rooms
have kitchenettes. Cash & credit
cards. Optional phone, cable TV.
Pets negotiable. Guest laundry.

Other

② CENTRALIA FACTORY OUTLETS
- London Fog
- Corning Revere
- Bass Shoes
- Over 25 other shops

⑪ CENTRALIA MARKET SQUARE
- Little Caesar's Pizza
- Bag & Save foods
- Sub Shop, Phone

⑮ HIT A TON INDOOR BATTING
  CAGES

⑯ FORT BORST PARK
- Restrooms, picnic area,
  children's play area,
  walking trail, historic
  home & fort, rhododendron
  garden. Very peaceful.

㉑ MINIT-LUBE

㉒ OUTLET MARKET PLACE
- Vanity Fair
- Many other shops

㉖ ROTARY RIVERSIDE PARK
- Camping, RV pump-out,
  covered picnic area,
  showers, restrooms,
  children's play area, &
  sports fields.

㉞ SAFEWAY MALL
- 6am - midnight
- Payless Drugs, Phone
- China Dragon Restaurant

Exit 88

This exit provides convenient access to Tenino and the South Sound Speedway, Aberdeen, and the Pacific coast beaches, via US Hwy 12.

Key Features: South Sound Speedway, 24-hour gas & food.

Towing:
JJ's Towing 736-2356
Charlie's Towing 736-4019

Northbound:

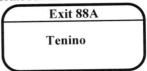

Southbound:

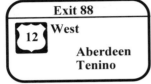

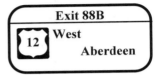

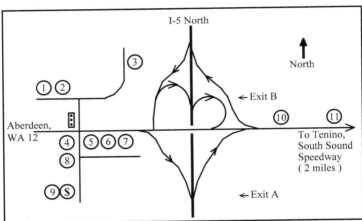

Service Stations

② **TEXACO**   24 Hrs.
Self-serve, large mini-mart, cash & credit cards, phones, no restrooms. Key-making shop in mini-mart.

④ **ARCO AM/PM**   24 Hrs.
Self-serve, mini-mart, cash & cash-machine cards, phone, restrooms.

⑤ **FRED'S DISCOUNT TIRES** 7am-8pm Mon-Sat, 8am-5pm Sun. Self- & full-serve, cash & credit cards, phone, restrooms. Propane.

⑪ **SPEEDWAY GROCERY** 5am-9pm Mon-Sat, 7am-8pm Sun. Self-serve, large mini-mart with a deli & a fax machine, cash & credit cards, phone, no restrooms. Kerosene, ice, an outside eating area, & fresh doughnuts daily.

Restaurants

① **LITTLE RED BARN** $$
24 Hrs. Full & counter service, featuring an American menu specializing in steak and chicken. Full bar. Cash & credit cards. Live music on Thur, Fri & Sat.

Exit 88 *continued*

⑦ **HACIENDA** $$
11am-9pm Mon-Thur, 11am-11pm Fri, 3pm-10pm Sat-Sun. Full-service restaurant featuring a Mexican menu. Full bar. Cash & credit cards, extensive truck parking.

Fast Food

⑧ **DAIRY QUEEN**

⑥ **BURGERMASTER**

Lodging

Other

③ **BUZZY'S TRUCK & DIESEL REPAIR**
- 7am-6pm Mon-Sat.

⑨ **THURSTON COUNTY SHERIFF'S OFFICE**

⑩ **FRANK'S RV REPAIR**
- 8am-5:30pm Mon-Fri, 8am-4pm Sat, closed Sun. 273-8591

Rest Area

Northbound: At mile-marker 90, the Scatter Creek Rest Area features:

- Free coffee
- Visitor Information
- Vending Machines
- Picnic area
- Phone

Southbound: At mile-marker 94, the Maytown Rest Area features:

- Free coffee
- Vending machines
- Picnic area
- Phone

Fort Borst Park, Exit 82

Exit 95

This exit is a good place to get off the freeway for a stretch and a bite to eat.

Key Features: Food and phone

Towing:
JJ's Towing 273-8481 or
736-2356

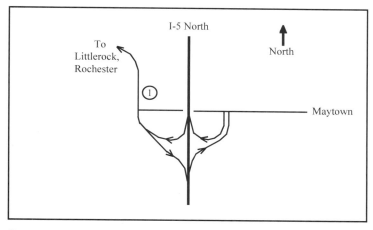

Restaurants

① **FARM BOY** $$
6am-8pm Mon-Sat, 7am-8pm
Sun. Cash & credit cards. Full
service American menu with a
drive-thru window. Specializing
in burgers and sandwiches.
Restrooms, outside picnic area,
phones.

Exit 99

This exit features a 24-hour truck stop with food and gas. State Highway 121 starts at this exit.

Key Features: 24-hour gas and food.

Towing:
Poages Towing 943-1531
Rick's Towing 352-0235

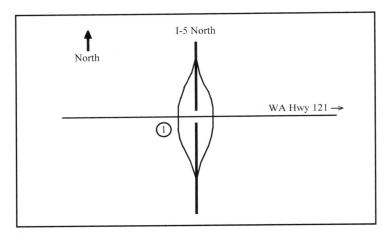

Service Stations

① **RESTOVER TRUCK STOP** 24 Hrs. Self-serve, mini-mart, cash & credit cards & checks, phone, ice, restrooms, diesel & propane. Extensive truck parking.

Restaurants

① **RESTOVER**
Food available at the Truck Stop. Restaurant was being remodeled at time of review.

Exit 101

This exit provides access to the Olympia Airport, food, and gas.

Key Features: Olympia Airport

Towing:
Poages Towing 943-1531

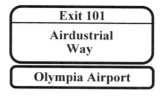

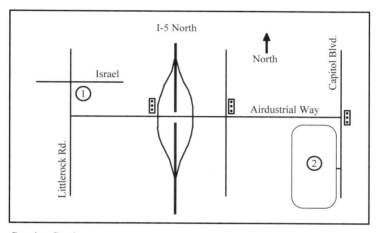

Service Stations

① **FRONTIER FOODS** 6:30-11pm,
7 days. Self-serve, large mini-
mart, cash & credit cards &
checks, no restrooms, phone.
This is really a grocery store that
sells gas.

Other

② **OLYMPIA AIRPORT**
The entrance to the airport
is two miles from the
exit.

Exit 102

This exit leads to the Southern part of Olympia and many services. It's closely linked to Exit 103 by Capitol Blvd and 2nd Ave. See Exit 103 for additional services.

Key Features: 24-hour gas, food, and lodging.

Towing: Poage's Towing 943-1531, Rick's Towing 352-0235

Northbound:

Exit 102
So. Tumwater **Black Lake**

Southbound:

Exit 102
Trosper Rd. **Black Lake**

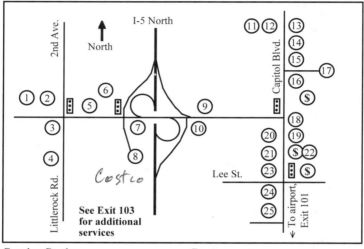

Service Stations

⑤ **CHEVRON** 24 Hrs.
Self-serve, mini-mart, cash & credit cards, restrooms, phone.

⑦ **BP** 24 Hrs.
Self-serve, tiny mini-mart, cash & credit cards, phone, handicapped restrooms. Mechanic on duty 8am-4:30pm Mon-Sat.

⑯ **TEXACO** 24 Hrs.
Self-serve, small mini-mart, cash & credit cards, handicapped restrooms, phone, diesel.

㉒ **7-11** 24 Hrs.
Self-serve, large mini-mart, cash & credit cards, cash machine, phone. No restrooms.

Restaurants

③ **IRON SKILLET** $$
6am-9pm Mon-Thurs, 6am-12am Fri, 7am-10pm Sat, 8am-8pm Sun. Cash & credit cards & checks. Full & counter service. American menu.

⑥ **NICKELBY'S** $$
6am-9pm Mon, 6am-10pm Tues-Thurs, 6am-11pm Fri, 7am-11pm Sat, 7am-9pm Sun. Full & counter service. American menu with salad bar & espresso. Cash & credit cards. Full bar. Live music on Fri & Sat.

Exit 102 *continued*

⑫ **HAPPY TERIYAKI V** $$
11am-10pm Mon-Sat, closed
Sun. Full-service Japanese
menu with take-out available.
Phone: 786-9107. Cash & credit
cards & checks. Beer.

㉑ **JIM'S DINER** $$
6am-10pm Mon-Thurs, Sat, Sun,
6am-11pm Fri. Full-service
American menu. Cash & credit
cards & checks. Gift shop.

Fast Food

⑨ **JACK IN THE BOX**

⑩ **ARBY'S** (outside phone)

⑬ **KFC**

⑭ **BREWERY CITY PIZZA**

⑮ **CATLIN'S**

⑱ **BURGER KING**

⑲ **PIZZA HUT**

㉓ **SUBWAY**

㉔ **MCDONALD'S**

Lodging

⑧ **TYEE HOTEL** ☺☺☺ $$$
1-800-648-6440, Local: 352-0511.
Non-smoking & handicapped
rooms available. Cash & credit
cards & checks. Discounts
available. Cable TV, phone.
Pets OK with fee. Outdoor
heated pool, tennis court,
basketball court, in-room spa.
Meeting rooms available.
Capitol airporter stops here.
Attached restaurant: *Sutter's.*
Breakfast, lunch, dinner. Dinner:
$$$, featuring steak & seafood.
Full bar. Live music in lounge.

⑰ **BEST WESTERN TUMWATER INN**
(206) 956-1235 ☺☺☺ $$$
Non-smoking & handicapped
rooms available. Some rooms
have kitchenettes, all rooms
have refrigerators. Some suites.
Cash & credit cards & company
checks. Discounts available.
Cable TV, phone. Pets OK with
fee. Coffee served in lobby.
Guest laundry.

Other

① **TUMWATER VETERINARY
HOSPITAL**

② **MEGA FOODS**
• 24 Hrs.
• Pharmacy
• Phone
• Cash machine

④ **CHARLIE'S R.V. WORLD**
• RV Sales & Service
• 7:30am-5:30pm Mon-Fri,
  7:30am-5pm Sat,
  closed Sun.
• 1-800-562-6008

⑪ **A J PET & WILDLIFE
CENTER**

⑳ **POAGE'S INC.**
• Towing & AAA Auto
  Repair
• 7:30am-5:30pm Mon-Fri.
• 943-1531

㉕ **GOODYEAR TIRES**
• 352-5322

Exit 103

This exit features the Olympic Brewery and a couple of lovely parks: Tumwater Falls Park and Capitol Lake/Marathon Park. If you have time, be sure to stop for a walk through Tumwater Falls Park, and don't miss the view of the capitol across Capitol Lake! This exit is closely linked to Exit 102 by Capitol Blvd and 2nd Ave. See Exit 102 for additional services.

Key Features: Olympic Brewery, Tumwater Falls Park, Capitol Lake/Marathon Park, gas and food.

Towing: Poage's Towing 943-1531

Northbound:

Exit 103
Deschutes Way

Southbound:

Exit 103
2nd Ave.

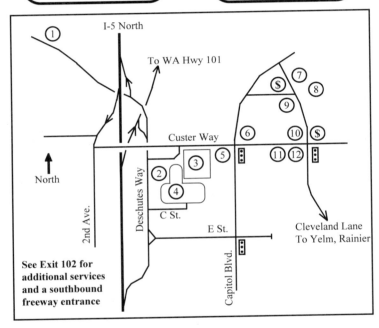

See Exit 102 for additional services and a southbound freeway entrance

Service Stations

⑨ **ARCO** 9am-6pm, 7 days. Self-serve, cash only.

⑫ **TEXACO** 24 Hrs. Self-serve, mini-mart, cash & credit cards, phone.

Restaurants

② **FALLS TERRACE** $$ 11am-9pm Mon-Fri, 11:30am-9pm Sat, 11:30am-8pm Sun. Cash & credit cards. Full service.

American menu featuring steak & seafood. Full bar. Overlooks Tumwater Falls: gorgeous view!

⑤ **SOUTH PACIFIC** $$ 11am-9pm Mon-Thurs, 11am-10pm Fri, 3pm-10pm Sat, 12pm-9pm Sun. Full-service. Chinese & Polynesian menu. Cash & credit cards & checks. Full bar. Take-out & delivery available. Phone: 352-0701.

Exit 103 *continued*

⑧ **MASON JAR** $$
9am-5pm Mon-Fri. Closed Sat-Sun. Features pasta, espresso.

Fast Food

⑥ **BASKIN-ROBBINS**

⑩ **BIG TOM'S**

Other

① **CAPITOL LAKE/MARATHON PARK**
• Gorgeous view of the capitol and downtown Olympia
• Picnic area
• Jogging trails
• Restrooms

③ **OLYMPIA BREWERY**
• Tours daily 8am-4:30pm

④ **TUMWATER FALLS PARK**
• Gorgeous walking trail along the Falls and river
• Picnic area
• 15-acre park
• Restrooms
• Children's play area

⑦ **SAFEWAY**
• 6am-midnight

⑪ **LAUNDROMAT**

Bridge decoration on Capitol Blvd., this exit.

Tumwater Falls Park, Exit 103.

Exit 104

This exit leads to US Hwy 101 and the Olympic Peninsula. There are no services near this exit.

Key Features: No services

Towing:
Poage's Towing 943-1531

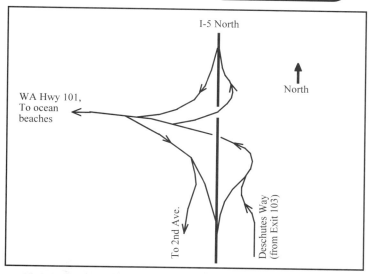

Exit 104
101 North
Aberdeen
Port Angles

I-5 North

North

WA Hwy 101,
To ocean
beaches

To 2nd Ave.

Deschutes Way
(from Exit 103)

Wooden statue of a State Highway worker on the grounds of the
City of Olympia Maintenance Center, Exit 105B

Exit 105 (Northbound)
Exit 105 A (Southbound)

This exit leads to the State Capitol and Olympia's city center.

Key Features: State Capitol, numerous services towards city center.

Towing: Jerry's Towing 943-8200; Howard's Towing 943-6644

Northbound:

Exit 105
State Capitol
City Center
Port of Olympia

Southbound:

Exit 105A
State Capitol
City Center

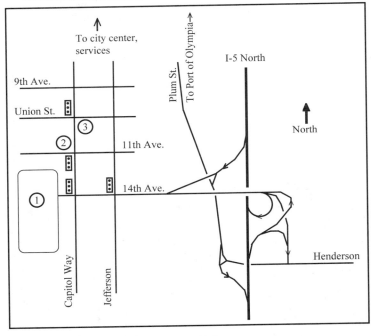

Restaurants

② SHANGHAI $$
11am-9:30pm Mon, 11am-10pm
Tues-Fri, 12pm-10pm Sat,
closed Sun. Full service. Cash
& credit cards. Chinese menu.
Full bar.

Fast Food

③ DAIRY QUEEN

Other

① STATE CAPITOL
Parking free on weekends.
Beautiful grounds for a stroll.

Wagner's Bakery
360-357.7268

Exit 105 B

This *Southbound-only* exit leads to the Port of Olympia. You can also reach the State Capitol from this exit. See Exit 105A for more information on the area adjacent to the Capitol.

Key Features: Port of Olympia

Towing:
Poage's Towing 943-1531
Howard's Towing 943-6644

> **Exit 105B**
>
> **Port of Olympia**

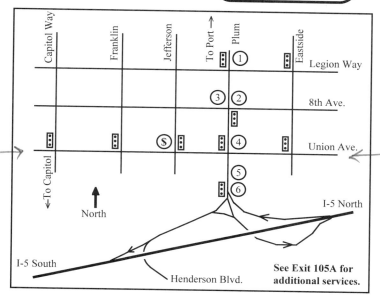

Service Stations

④ **CHEVRON** 24 Hrs. Self- & full-serve. Mechanic on duty 7am-6pm Mon-Fri, 8am-4:30pm Sat. Cash & credit cards. Restrooms, phone, ice, espresso, propane.

Restaurants

② **CASA MIA** $$
11am-11pm Sun-Thurs, 11am-12am Fri-Sat. Full service with take-out available. Italian menu & deli. Espresso booth outside. Cash & credit cards. Full bar.

⑤ **CRYSTAL PALACE II** $$
6am-10am Mon-Fri breakfast, 11am-9pm Mon-Sat, closed Sun.

Cash & credit cards. Full service. Chinese menu with steak and seafood. Full bar. Live music on Fri, Sat.

Fast Food

① **JACK IN THE BOX**
③ **MCDONALD'S**

Lodging

⑥ **CARRIAGE INN** ☺☺☺ $$$
(206) 943-4710 Cash & credit cards, discounts available. Cable TV, phone, refrigerators in all rooms. Handicapped & non-smoking rooms available. No pets. Free coffee in lobby. Continental breakfast. Fax available. Outdoor heated pool.

Exit 107

This exit features emergency services, various places to eat, and service stations. See exit 108 for additional services.

Key Features: Hospital, food, and gas.

Towing:
Rick's Towing 352-0235
South Sound Towing 943-6336

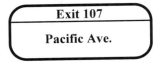

Exit 107

Pacific Ave.

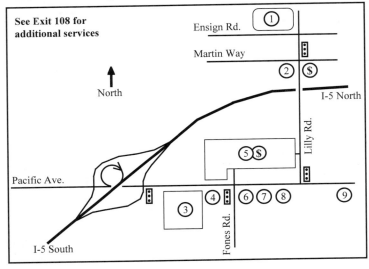

See Exit 108 for additional services

Ensign Rd. ①

Martin Way

North

② ⑤

I-5 North

Lilly Rd.

⑤ ⑤

Pacific Ave.

④ ⑥ ⑦ ⑧ ⑨

③

Fones Rd.

I-5 South

Service Stations

② **7-11 (Citgo)** 24 Hrs.
Self-serve, large mini-mart, cash & credit cards, phone.

⑦ **Texaco** 24 Hrs.
Self-serve, tiny mini-mart, cash & credit cards, diesel, restrooms with handicapped access, phone.

⑨ **Chevron** 24 Hrs.
Self-serve, large mini-mart, cash & credit cards, restrooms, phone.

Fast Food

④ **Shari's**
⑤ **Izzy's Pizza**
⑤ **Madrid's Espresso**
⑤ **Figaro's Pizza**
⑥ **Taco Time**

Other

① **St. Peter Hospital**

③ **Ross Olympia Square**
  • Ross
  • Pacific Linen
  • Sizzler

⑤ **Olympia Square**
  • Food pavillion, 24-Hrs.
  • Izzy's Pizza
  • Kinko's Copies
  • Madrid's Espresso
  • Maytag laundry
  • Figaro's Pizza
  • Yukio's Teriyaki
  • United Postal (fax, UPS)
  • Phone

⑧ **Veterinary Clinic**
  (456-6006)

Former Officer's Quarters on Fort Vancouver, Exit 1B

Exit 108

This exit features 24-hour food and gas, as well as two large shopping malls. It is closely tied to Exit 109 via Martin Way and to Exit 107 via Pacific Ave. See Exits 107 and 109 for additional services.

Key Features: 24-hour food and gas, shopping.

Towing: Rick's Towing 352-0235; Lacey Collision & Towing 456-5401

Northbound:

> ### Exit 108
> **Sleater-Kinney Rd.**
> **College St.**

Southbound:

> ### Exit 108
> **Sleater-Kinney**
> **Rd. S.**

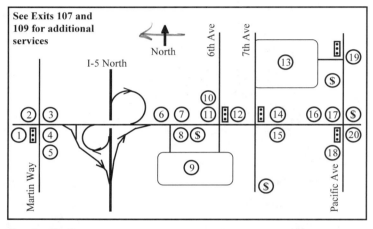

Service Stations

② **Unocal 76**   6am-11pm Mon-Fri, 7am-11pm Sat & Sun. Full- & self-serve, cash & credit cards, phone. Mechanic on duty 8am-7pm Mon & Wed, 8am-6pm Tues, Thur, & Fri., 8am-4pm Sat.

③ **Arco am/pm**   24 Hrs. Self-serve, mini-mart, cash & cash-machine cards, no restrooms, phones.

④ **Shell**   24 Hrs. Self-serve, mini-mart with hot food & inside seating, cash & credit cards, no restrooms, phones.

⑧ **Texaco**   24 Hrs. Self-serve, small mini-mart, cash & credit cards, phone, handicapped restrooms, diesel.

⑳ **Texaco** 6:30am-12am Mon-Sat, 7am-11pm Sun. Self-serve, large mini-mart, cash & credit cards, no restrooms, phone, ice.

Restaurants

⑤ **El Serape** $$ 11am-11pm Mon-Thur, 11am-12am Fri-Sat. noon-10pm Sun. Cash & credit cards. Full service. Mexican menu. Full bar.

Exit 108 *continued*

⑩ **RED CORAL** $$
11am-10pm Sun-Fri, 11am-
10:30pm Sat. 459-5500. Cash &
credit cards. Buffet service and
drive-thru take-out available.
Chinese menu with all-you-can-
eat salad bar. Beer & wine.

Fast Food

① **JACK IN THE BOX**
⑥ **MCDONALD'S**
⑦ **WENDY'S**
⑪ **ARBY'S**
⑫ **GODFATHER'S PIZZA**
⑭ **BASKIN-ROBBINS**
⑮ **WINCHELL'S DONUTS**
⑯ **PIETRO'S PIZZA**
⑲ **DAIRY QUEEN**

Other

⑨ **SOUTH SOUND CENTER**
  • 10am-9pm Mon-Fri,
    10am-6pm Sat,
    11am-6pm Sun.
  • Sears
  • Mervyn's
  • Nordstrom
  • Woolworth's
  • PetsMart
  • La Palma II Restaurant
  • Numerous other
    restaurants & shops
  • Phones
⑬ **MARKET SQUARE**
  • Fred Meyer
  • Oskar's German Deli
  • Hero At Large Sandwiches
⑰ **MINIT-LUBE**
⑱ **BRIG O'DUNE PET CENTER**

Exit 109

This exit features lodging, 24-hour gas and food, and several community colleges. It is very closely tied to Exits 107 and 108 via Martin Way and Sleater-Kinney Road. See Exits 107 and 108 for additional services.

Key Features: Gas, food, lodging, & St. Martin's College.

Towing: Rick's Towing 352-0235; Lacey Towing 491-9692

Northbound:

┌─────────────────────┐
│ **Exit 109** │
│ **Martin Way** │
└─────────────────────┘

Southbound:

┌─────────────────────┐
│ **Exit 109** │
│ **Martin Way** │
│ **Sleater-Kinney Rd. N.** │
└─────────────────────┘

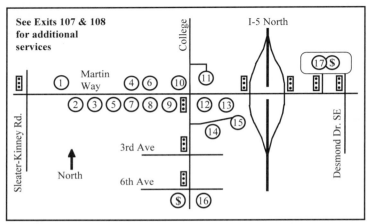

Service Stations

⑩ **TEXACO**   24 Hrs.
Self-serve, mini-mart, cash & credit cards, wheelchair-accessible restrooms, phone, diesel, drive-thru car wash, ice.

⑫ **BP**   24 Hrs.
Self-serve, mini-mart, cash & credit cards, restrooms, phone.

Restaurants

③ **MANDARIN HOUSE** $$
(206) 438-3388. 11am-9pm Tues-Thurs, 11am-10pm Fri, 12pm-10pm Sat, 12pm-9pm Sun, closed Mon. Full service. Chinese menu. Full bar. Cash & credit cards & checks.

⑥ **CASA MIA** $$
11:30am-11pm Mon-Thurs, 11:30am-12am Fri-Sat, 12pm-10pm Sun. Full-service. Cash & credit cards. Italian menu.

Fast Food

② **BURGER KING**
⑦ **BREWERY CITY PIZZA**
⑧ **ESPRESSO & DELI**
⑨ **SHARI'S**
⑬ **DENNY'S**

Exit 109 *continued*

Lodging

⑪ COMFORT INN ☺☺☺ $$$
456-6300 or 1-800-221-2222.
Cash & credit cards & checks,
discounts available. 30% senior
discount if reservations are
made via the 800 number.
Cable TV, phone, elevators.
King suites have microwave
and refrigerator. Handicapped
& non-smoking rooms available.
No pets. Continental breakfast
in office with tables and a
comfortable eating area. Indoor
heated pool, sauna, & exercise
area.

⑭ CAPITOL INN ☺☺☺ $$$
(206) 493-1991 Cash & credit
cards & checks, discounts &
weekly rates available. Cable
TV with Showtime, phone,
refrigerators & microwaves in
all rooms. Handicapped & non-
smoking rooms available. Some
kitchenettes. Pets OK with fee.
Free coffee in lobby. Fax
available. Sauna & exercise
area. Customer laundry.

⑮ SUPER 8 ☺☺ $$
(206) 459-8888 Cash & credit
cards & checks, Super 8 VIP
discount available. Cable TV,
phone. Handicapped & non-
smoking rooms available.
Indoor pool & spa. Pets OK
with fee. Free coffee in lobby.
Guest laundry. Conference
room available. Sea-Tac
Airporter service available.

Other

① WASHINGTON STATE PATROL
④ CAR WASH
⑤ COOPER'S TIRES
⑯ ST. MARTIN'S ABBEY &
   COLLEGE
⑰ MARTIN VILLAGE
   • Taco Bell
   • Mitzel's
   • ShopKo
   • Smith's
   • HomeBase
   • Discount Tire Co.

Exit 111

This exit leads to Tolmie State Park, numerous 24-hour facilities, and provides easy on-and-off access if you need a quick stop.

Key Features: 24-hour gas and diesel, 24-hour food, but no nearby lodging.

Towing:
Rick's Towing 352-0235
Nisqually Towing 491-1755

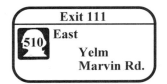

Exit 111
510 East
Yelm
Marvin Rd.

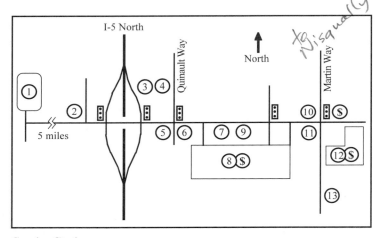

Service Stations

④ **BP FOOD MART**   24 Hrs.
Self-serve, large mini-mart (with 16 flavors of ice cream!), cash & credit cards, restrooms, phone. Diesel for professional truckers only.

⑤ **CHEVRON**   24 Hrs.
Self-serve, mini-mart, cash & credit cards, phone, restrooms accommodate wheelchairs.

⑥ **TEXACO**   24 Hrs.
Self-serve, large mini-mart, cash & credit cards, restrooms, phone, diesel, drive-thru car wash.

⑩ **ARCO DELI-MART**   24 Hrs.
Self-serve, large mini-mart, cash & credit cards, restrooms, phone, diesel.

⑪ **BP**   24 Hrs.
Self-serve, mini-mart, cash & credit cards, phone, restrooms

Restaurants

② **COUNTRY JUNCTION** $$
6am-9pm Mon-Fri, 7am-9pm Sat-Sun. Cash & credit cards. Counter & full service. American menu with take-out available. Specializing in breakfast items, burgers, & sandwiches. Most menu items under $6.

③ **HAWK'S PRAIRIE INN** $$
24 Hrs. 7 days. Counter & full-service. American menu featuring seafood, steak, & pasta. Cash & credit cards & checks. Full bar. Friendly, with a large fireplace & small gift area.

Exit 111 *continued*

Fast Food

⑦ **Dairy Queen**
⑨ **McDonald's**

Other

① **Tolmie State Park**
8am-dusk. Closed Mon &
Tue. On Nisqually beach, it
has kitchens & restrooms, but
no camping allowed. Five (5)
miles from the exit. Follow
signs west to Park. When
returning to I-5, take a left at
the only Stop sign (the I-5
intersection is not marked).

⑧ **Shopping Mall**
- Safeway (24 Hrs.)
- Payless Drugs
- Ben Franklin
- phone

⑫ **Hawk's Prairie Shopping Center**
- Thriftway (24 Hrs.)
- Oriental Garden Restaurant
- Phone
- True Value Hardware
- Shoe Repair
- Cleaners
- Ice

⑬ **Martin Way Mobile Home and RV Park**
- Adults 55 & older only.
- laundry
- no pets

Exit 114

This exit features the Nisqually National Wildlife Refuge and the Nisqually RV Park.

Key Features: Gas, food, and a quiet place to stop.

Towing: Nisqually Towing 491-1755; Lacey Collison & Towing 456-5400

Northbound:

Exit 114
Nisqually
Old Nisqually

Southbound:

Exit 114
Nisqually

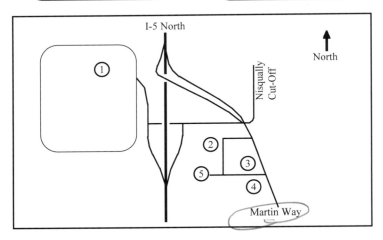

Service Stations

③ **SHELL** 6am-12am Mon-Fri, 7am-12am Sat-Sun. Self- & full-serve, cash & credit cards & checks, ice, phone, restrooms, propane. Mechanic on duty during normal station hours.

④ **TEXACO** 6am-10pm Mon-Fri, 7am-10pm Sat, 8am-10pm Sun. (206) 491-3831 Self-serve, large mini-mart, cash & credit cards, restrooms, phone, ice. Ice cream parlor & office for the RV park in the same building.

Restaurants

② **TINY'S BURGERHOUSE & GIFT SHOP** $ Cash & credit cards. Full service. American menu specializing in burgers &
sandwiches. Counter & take-out available. Large gift shop.

Other

① **NISQUALLY NATIONAL WILDLIFE REFUGE**
• Fee for entry

⑤ **NISQUALLY PLAZA RV PARK** (206) 491-3831 (Office in the Texaco Station)
• Telephone hook-ups
• HBO & cable TV
• Fishing & boat launch
• Playground
• Pool
• Coin-operated showers
• Laundry and rest rooms

Exit 116

This exit features the Fort Lewis Golf Course, but *no services.*

Key Features: A quiet place to stop and change drivers.

Northbound:

Exit 116
Mounts Road

Southbound:

Exit 116
Mounts Road
Old Nisqually

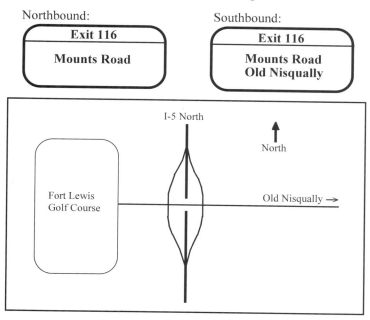

Airplane on a pedestal at Camp Murray, Exit 122.

Truck Weigh Station

Northbound: At mile marker 117, this weigh station has phones. No other services.

Gas station changing it's brand at Exit 212. Keep track of changes with the next edition of our book!

Exit 119

This exit provides access to Fort Lewis, North Fort Lewis, a small grocery store, and a long quiet street next to an open field - great for walking the dog!

CAUTION: When exiting Southbound, check for trains before turning right.

Key Features: Fort Lewis

Towing:
Nisqually Towing 491-1755
Lakewood Towing 582-5080

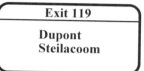

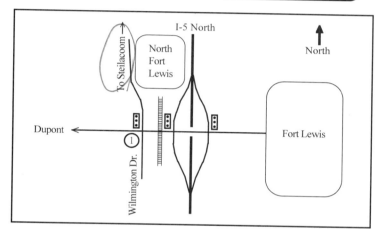

Other

① **DUPONT GROCERY & DELI**
6am- 9pm Mon-Thur,
6am-10pm Fri,
7am-10pm Sat,
8am- 9pm Sun.
• Phone
• Ice

Exit 120

This exit provides access to Fort Lewis, North Fort Lewis, and the Fort Lewis Military Museum. If you aren't going to Fort Lewis, don't get off here!

Key Features: Fort Lewis

Exit 120
Fort Lewis **No. Fort Lewis**

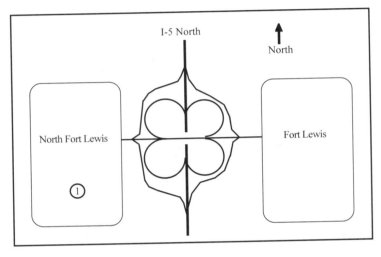

Other

① **FORT LEWIS MILITARY MUSEUM**
Open noon to 4 pm, closed, Monday and Tuesday.

Fort Lewis Military Museum.

Exit 122

This exit connects with Exit 123 via Union Ave, through the town of Tillicum. See Exit 123 for additional services.

Key Features: 24-hour gas and food.

Towing:
Lakewood Towing 582-5080

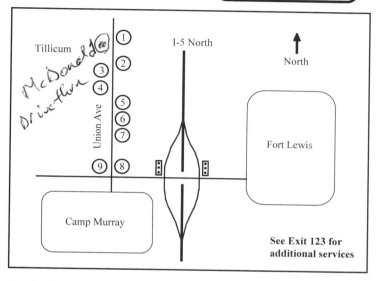

Service Stations

⑨ **ARCO AM/PM**   24 Hrs.
Self-serve, tiny mini-mart, cash & cash-machine cards, phone, restrooms. AAA Emergency Service, mechanic on duty 9am-6:30pm Mon-Sat. AAA Towing: 1-800-637-2010.

Restaurants

⑧ **GALLOPING GERTIE'S** $$
6am-10pm Sun-Thur, 6am-3am Fri-Sat. Cash & credit cards & checks. American menu. Counter, full service, & take-out available. Full bar.

Fast Food

② **SUBWAY**
③ **BASKIN-ROBBINS**
④ **KENTUCKY FRIED CHICKEN**
⑤ **TACO BELL**
⑦ **BURGER AND SHAKE STOP**

Other

① **COIN-OP CAR WASH**
⑥ **7-11** (cash machine in store)

Exit 123

This exit connects with Exit 122 via Union Ave through the town of Tillicum. See Exit 122 for additional services.

Key Features: 24-hour gas and food.

Towing: Lakewood Towing 582-5080

Northbound:

Exit 123
Thorne Lane

Southbound:

Exit 123
Tillicum

I-5 North

4 lanes

North

Thorne Lane

Union Ave

3 lanes

Fort Lewis Logistics Center

① ② ③ ④

Tillicum

See Exit 122 for additional services

Restaurants

③ CHING HA $$
11am-12:30am Sun-Thur, 11am-1:30am Fri-Sat. Cash & credit cards. Chinese Mandarin menu. Full service, counter service, & take-out available.

Fast Food

② DOMINO'S PIZZA
④ SUBSHOP

Other

① TILLICUM LAUNDROMAT
• 8am-10pm 7 days

Exit 124

This exit provides access to McChord AFB and Lakewood, as well as numerous small restaurants, motels, and bars catering mostly to local clientele. This exit connects to Exit 125 via Pacific Hwy SW. See Exit 125 for additional services.

Key Features: 24-hour gas and car repair.

Towing:
Bill's Towing 458-5963
Parkland Towing 535-0572

```
Exit 124

Gravelly
Lake Dr.
```

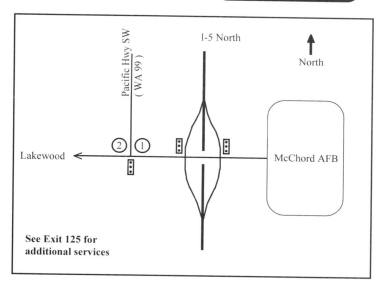

Service Stations

① **BP**   24 Hrs.
Self- & full-serve, cash & credit cards, restrooms, phone. Full-service mechanic on duty 7am-10pm 7 days.

② **Arco am/pm**   24 Hrs.
Self-serve, cash & cash-machine cards. No restrooms. Phone, soda vending machines.

Exit 125

This exit provides plenty of lodging and food, along with medical services and the Lakewood Mall. There are many services available further west toward Lakewood that are not shown on this map. This exit also connects to Exit 124, via southbound Pacific Hwy SW. See Exit 124 for additional services.

Key Features: 24-hour gas, diesel, food, & lodging.

Towing: Tacoma Valley Towing 582-6300 or 863-1000, Lakewood Towing 582-5080

Exit 125
Lakewood McChord AFB

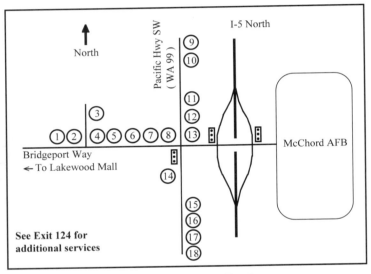

Service Stations

⑬ **Unocal 76** 24 Hrs. Self- & full-serve, cash & credit cards, phone, restrooms, diesel, propane. Mechanic on duty 9am-9pm, 7 days a week. Mechanic takes checks.

Restaurants

④ **Leslie's** $$ 24 hours, 7 days. Cash & credit cards. Counter & full service. American menu with take-out available. Full bar. Ample parking. Live country music in lounge.

Fast Food

⑥ **Madeleine's Drive-Thru**

⑦ **Kentucky Fried Chicken**

⑫ **Denny's**

Lodging

⑨ **Home Motel** ☺ $$ (206) 584-1717 Kitchenettes & refrigerators available. Cash & credit cards. Discounts available. Cable TV, phone. No pets. Laundry.

Exit 125 *continued*

⑩ **ROSE GARDEN MOTEL** ☺ $$
(206) 584-2840 Non-smoking
rooms, kitchenettes with
refrigerator available. Cash &
credit cards. Discounts available.
Cable TV, phone. No pets.

⑪ **LAKEWOOD LODGE** ☺ $$
(206) 588-4443 Kitchenettes
with refrigerators available.
Cash & credit cards. Discounts
& weekly rates available. Cable
TV, phone. No pets. Rustic,
relaxed setting: our choice for
lodging near the freeway at this
exit.

⑯ **MADIGAN MOTEL** ☺ $$
Cash & credit cards. Cable TV,
phone. Continental breakfast,
guest laundry, children's play
area. *Attached Restaurant:*
Mory's 24 Hrs.

⑰ **COLONIAL MOTEL** ☺ $$
(206) 581-1544 Kitchenettes
with refrigerator available.
Cash & credit cards. Discounts
available. Cable TV, phone.
Pets OK with no fee. Waterbeds.
Free coffee in office.

⑱ **FT. LEWIS MOTEL** ☺ $$
(206) 588-7226 Kitchenettes
with refrigerator available.
Cash & credit cards. Discounts
& weekly rates available. Cable
TV, phone. No pets. Laundry.

Other

① **ST. CLARE HOSPITAL**
② **THE PET DOCTOR**
③ **COIN-OP LAUNDRY**
⑤ **LAKEWOOD CAR WASH**
⑧ **U-HAUL**
• Propane
⑭ **PRECISION TUNE-UP**
• 582-3338
⑮ **WALT'S**
• Radiator, muffler, &
brake repair

Exit 127

This exit is a great place to grab a bite to eat or for an extended stay near McChord AFB, especially for airplane buffs who might want to watch the planes taking off and landing.

Key Features: 24-hour gas, food, and lodging.

Towing:
Gene's Towing 588-1757
Lakewood Towing 582-5080

Exit 127
East
512
Puyallup
Mt. Rainier

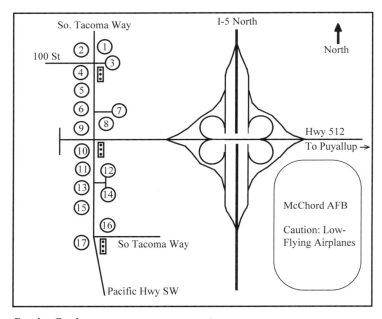

Service Stations

④ **ARCO AM/PM**   24 Hrs.
Self-serve, mini-mart, cash & cash-machine cards, phone, restrooms.

⑧ **TEXACO**   24 Hrs.
Self-serve, mini-mart, cash & credit cards, phone, diesel, drive-thru car wash. No restrooms.

⑩ **BP**   24 Hrs.
Self-serve, mini-mart, cash & credit cards, restrooms with wheelchair access, phone.

⑯ **ARCO AM/PM**   5am-12am Mon-Fri, 6am-12am Sat, 7am-12am Sun. Self-serve, mini-mart, cash & cash-machine cards, phone, restrooms.

Restaurants

⑦ **BILLY MCHALE'S** $$
11am-10pm Mon-Thur, 11am-11pm Fri, 11:30am-11pm Sat, 11:30am-10pm Sun. (206)582-6330 Cash & credit cards & checks. Full service. American menu with take-out available. Full bar. Lots of atmosphere, complete with an airplane hanging from the ceiling!

Exit 127 *continued*

⑪ **DaHaRi Oriental Buffet** $$
11am-9pm 7 days a week. (206)
581-0606 Chinese buffet. Cash
& credit cards & checks. Very
friendly, with lots of parking.

⑰ **Mazatlan** $$
11am-10pm Sun-Thur, 11am-
11pm Fri-Sat. (206) 588-8817
Full service with take-out
available. Cash & credit cards
& checks. Mexican menu with
full bar. Lots of parking.

Fast Food

⑤ **Dairy Queen**

⑥ **Ivar's Seafood**

⑨ **Sizzler**

⑫ **McDonald's**

⑬ **Frisko Freeze**

⑭ **Taco Time**

⑮ **Subway**

Lodging

① **Budget Inn** Reviewers
not permitted to see rooms. $$
(206) 588-6615 Kitchenettes &
waterbeds available, cash &
credit cards. Discounts &
weekly & monthly rates
available. Cable TV, phone.
Pets OK with fee. Free coffee,
tea, & donuts in office.

② **Western Inn** ☺☺ $$
(206) 588-5241 Non-smoking
rooms, refrigerator / kitchenette
available. Cash & credit cards.
Many discounts available,
weekly & monthly rates. Cable
TV, phone. No pets. Coffee
served in lobby. *Attached
Restaurant:* Jim Moore's:
breakfast, lunch, & dinner, $$,
full bar.

③ **Vagabond Inn** ☺ $$
(206) 581-2920 Non-smoking
rooms, refrigerators & kitchenettes available. Cash & credit
cards. Discounts available,
weekly rates. TV, phone. No
pets. Some covered parking.
Old-fashioned motel, but a
bargain. Room we viewed had a
separate sitting area.

Exit 128

This is a *Northbound* exit only, closely tied to Exit 129 via both Hosmer Street and Tacoma Mall Blvd. Check Exit 129 for additional nearby services. Most hotels at this exit offer military and government discounts to accommodate visitors to McChord AFB and Ft. Lewis.

Key Features: 24-hour gas, food, and lodging.

Towing:
Bill's Towing 272-9393
Lakewood Towing 582-5080

Exit 128

So. 84 St.

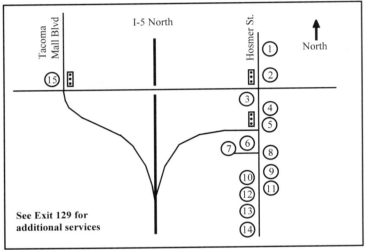

See Exit 129 for additional services

Service Stations

② **BP**   6am-12pm 7 days/wk
Self- & full-serve, tiny mini-mart, cash & credit cards, phone. No restrooms. Mechanic available for flat repair, minor maintenance.

④ **CHEVRON**   24 Hrs.
Self-serve, mini-mart, cash & credit cards, phone, restrooms accommodate wheelchairs.

⑤ **TEXACO**   24 Hrs.
Self-serve, mini-mart, cash & credit cards, restrooms, phone, diesel.

⑮ **ARCO AM/PM**   24 Hrs.
Self-serve, mini-mart, cash & cash-machine cards, phone, restrooms.

Restaurants

① **CHINA TOWN** $$
11am-10pm Mon-Thur, 11am-12pm Fri-Sat. Buffet with take-out available, cash & credit cards. Chinese menu. Full bar. Lots of parking.

⑧ **PIZZA ROMA** $$
10:30am-12am Mon-Thur, 10:30am-1am Fri-Sat, 12pm-12am Sun. (206) 531-6000 Full service with take-out & delivery available. Cash & credit cards & checks. Beer.

Exit 128 *continued*

⑨ **TK** $$
11:00am-4am Mon-Sat, 2pm-4am Sun. Full & counter service available. Cash & credit cards. Korean menu. Beer.

⑬ **COPPERFIELD'S** $$$
6:30am-10:30pm Mon-Fri, 7:30am-11pm Sat-Sun. (206) 531-1500 Full service with take-out available, cash & credit cards & checks. American menu with Italian entrees. Full bar.

Fast Food

⑦ **DENNY'S**

Lodging

③ **SHERWOOD INN**   Reviewers not permitted to see rooms. $$ (206) 535-2800 Non-smoking rooms & refrigerators available. Cash & credit cards & checks. Discounts available. Cable TV, phone, elevators. Pets OK. Safe deposit boxes, seasonal outdoor pool. Shuttle service is available to Sea-Tac airport. Thrifty car rental on site. *Attached restaurant:* Sherwood Gardens Cafe & lounge, $$, full bar.

⑥ **ROTHEM INN**   ☺ $$
(206) 535-0123 Non-smoking & handicapped rooms. Cash & credit cards. Weekly rates available. Cable TV, phone. No pets. Coffee in lobby.

⑩ **HOWARD JOHNSON LODGE**
1-800-IGO-HOJO ☺☺ $$$
local: 535-3100 Non-smoking & handicapped rooms. Cash & credit cards & checks. Discounts available. Cable TV, phone. No pets. Seasonal outdoor pool. Continental breakfast served in lobby, coffee in rooms.

⑫ **BEST WESTERN TACOMA INN**
(206) 535-2880   ☺☺☺ $$$
Non-smoking rooms, refrigerators, & kitchenettes available. Cash & credit cards & checks. Discounts available. Cable TV, phone. Pets OK with fee. Heated outdoor pool, exercise area, putting green, children's play area. Laundry open for guests. Coffee in room.

⑭ **TRAVELODGE** ☺☺☺ $$$
1-800-255-3050, local: 539-1153 Non-smoking rooms, refrigerators & microwaves available. Cash & credit cards & checks. Many discounts available. Cable TV, phone, metal security doors, recliners in some rooms. Seasonal outdoor pool. Shuttle service available to Sea-Tac airport. Continental breakfast.

Other

⑪ **MAYTAG LAUNDROMAT**

Exit 129

This exit features quiet, easy-to-get-to Wapato Park, just off the freeway. Great places to stop for lunch or dinner and a much-needed break. Services for Exits 128 and 130 are easily accessible from this exit, via Hosmer Street and Tacoma Mall Blvd.

Key Features: 24-hour food, gas, and lodging.

Towing: Gene's Towing 588-1757
Tacoma Valley Towing 582-6300 or 863-1000

Northbound: Southbound:

Exit 129	**Exit 129**
So. 72 St.	**So. 72 St.**
	So. 84 St.

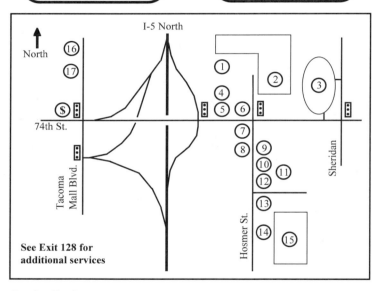

See Exit 128 for
additional services

Service Stations

⑦ **ARCO AM/PM**   24 Hrs.
Self-serve, mini-mart, cash & cash-machine cards, phone, restrooms.

Restaurants

① **OLIVE GARDEN** $$
11am-10pm Mon-Fri, 11am-11pm Sat-Sun. (206) 475-1772. Full service with take-out available. Italian menu. Cash & credit cards & checks. Full bar. Lots of parking.

② **MONGOLIAN GRILL** $$
11:30am-9:30pm Mon-Thur, 11:30am-10pm Fri, noon-10pm Sat, noon-9:30 Sun. (206) 475-0778 Full-service & buffet Chinese menu featuring a unique buffet stir-fry counter. Take-out available. Beer & wine. Cash & credit cards & checks. If you'd like to try a stir-fry combination to suit your mood, this is a must-stop restaurant. Located in the Tacoma Place Mall.

Exit 129 *continued*

⑤ RED LOBSTER $$
11am-10pm Sun-Thur, 11am-11pm Fri-Sat. (206) 474-1262 Full service. Seafood menu. Cash & credit cards & checks. Full bar.

⑨ ELMER'S $$
6am-10pm Sun-Thur, 6am-11pm Fri-Sat. (206) 473-0855 Full service with take-out available. Cash & credit cards & checks. Full bar. American menu specializing in pancakes & steaks. Breakfast, lunch, & dinner served all day.

⑭ MITZEL'S $$
6am-11pm Sun-Thur, 6am-12am Fri-Sat. (206) 472-8426 Full service with take-out available. Cash & credit cards & checks. Beer & wine. American menu specializing in pies & fresh turkey.

⑰ CALZONES $$
7am-10pm Mon-Thur, 7am-11pm Fri-Sat, 8am-9pm Sun. (206) 475-3715 Full service with take-out, delivery, & catering available. Cash & credit cards & checks. Full bar. Italian menu. Delivery phone: 475-3006.

Fast Food

② TACO BELL
② SUB SHOP
② STARBUCKS COFFEE
④ DAIRY QUEEN
⑥ SHARI'S
⑩ BURGER KING
⑫ INTERNATIONAL HOUSE OF PANCAKES
⑬ JACK IN THE BOX
⑯ ROUND TABLE PIZZA

Lodging

⑧ SHILO INN ☺☺☺ $$$
1-800-222-2244 Non-smoking rooms, refrigerators, & kitchenettes available. Elevators. Cash & credit cards & checks. Discounts available. Cable TV, phone. Pets OK with fee. Indoor pool with spa & exercise area. Laundry for guests. Continental breakfast, complimentary apples, coffee, & popcorn.

⑪ MOTEL 6 ☺ $$
(206) 473-7100 Non-smoking rooms available. Cash & credit cards. Cable TV, phone, bathtubs. Pets OK. Seasonal outdoor pool & spa.

⑯ DAYS INN ☺☺☺ $$$
(206) 475-5900 Non-smoking rooms & refrigerators available. Cash & credit cards & checks. Discounts available. Cable TV, phone. Pets OK with fee. Seasonal outdoor pool. Guest membership at nearby Tacoma Athletic Club for $2/day. Attractive lobby & grounds, complimentary apples & newspapers. Covered walkway to Calzones Restaurant.

Other

② TACOMA PLACE MALL
 • Starbucks Coffee
 • Little Tokyo Teriyaki
 • HomeBase
 • SportMart
 • Taco Bell
 • Phones

③ WAPATO PARK

⑮ TACOMA SOUTH CENTER
 • Mega Foods (24 Hrs.)
 • Drug Emporium
 • Round Table Pizza
 • Car Tec
 • Tacoma South Cinemas

Exit 130

This exit features the Tacoma Mall, one of the largest malls in the Puget Sound area, and 24-hour services, including diesel. Chuck E Cheese is a great place for kids to let off some steam!

Key Features: Tacoma Mall and Chuck E Cheese

Towing: Gene's Towing 588-1757

Northbound:

Exit 130
So. 56 St. **Tac. Mall Blvd.**

Southbound:

Exit 130
So. 56 St.

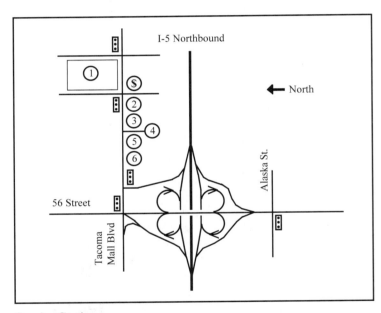

Service Stations

⑥ **TEXACO**   24 Hrs.
Self-serve, mini-mart, cash & credit cards, restrooms, phone, diesel. Drive-thru car wash.

Restaurants

② **EL TORITO** $$
11am-10pm Mon-Thur, 11am-11pm Fri-Sat, 10am-10pm Sun. (206) 473-7676   Full service with take-out available. Cash & credit cards & checks. Mexican menu. Full bar. Good food.

③ **CHUCK E CHEESE** $$
11am-9pm Sun-Thur, 11am-10pm Fri-Sat. Good pizza & salad bar. Take-out available. Cash & credit cards & checks. GREAT place for the kids to let off some steam! Lots of activity games and animated entertainment for children, from toddler to teen.

Exit 130 *continued*

⑤ **TONY ROMA'S** $$
11am-11pm Sun-Thur, 11am-
12pm Fri-Sat. (206) 473-7152
Full service with take-out &
delivery available. Cash &
credit cards & checks. BBQ
ribs & chicken a specialty. Full
bar.

Fast Food

④ **SUBWAY**

Other

① **TACOMA MALL**
   9:30am-9:30pm Mon-Sat,
   11am-6pm Sun
   • JC Penny
   • Nordstrom
   • Payless Drug
   • Mervyn's
   • Bon Marche
   • Sears
   • Noah's Pet & Hobby
   • 10 restaurants
   • Cash machine
   • Dozens of other stores

Exit 132

This exit provides access to 38th Street or State Hwy 16. Hwy 16 leads to the Pt. Defiance Zoo and the Olympic Peninsula via the Tacoma Narrows Bridge. The map below is *only* for the 38th St. portion of this exit.

Key Features: 24-hour gas, variety of food, and access to malls.

Towing:
Bill's Towing 272-9393
Gene's Towing 588-1757

Northbound:

Exit 132	
West **16** **Gig Harbor** **Bremerton**	**So. 38th St**

Southbound:

Exit 132	
So. 38th St	**West** **16** **Gig Harbor** **Bremerton**

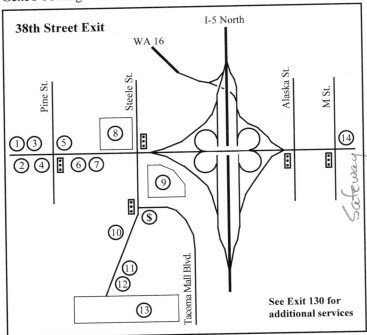

38th Street Exit

I-5 North

WA 16

Pine St.

Steele St.

Alaska St.

M St.

Safeway

① ③ ⑤ ⑧ ⑭
② ④ ⑥ ⑦
⑨
$
⑩
⑪
⑫
⑬

Tacoma Mall Blvd.

See Exit 130 for additional services

Service Stations

⑤ **ARCO AM/PM** 24 Hrs. Self-serve, cash & cash-machine cards, restrooms, phone.

⑭ **TEXACO** 24 Hrs. (206) 0272 Self- & full-serve, mini-mart, cash & credit cards, restrooms. Mechanic available for minor repairs Mon-Sat.

Restaurants

⑨ **RED ROBIN** $$ 11am-12am Mon-Fri, 11am-1am Sat, 9am-12am Sun. Full service with take-out available. Cash & credit cards. American menu, specializing in meal-size burgers. Full bar. Good food & atmosphere.

Exit 132 *continued*

⑨ **AZTECA** $$
11am-10:30pm Sun-Thur,
11am-11:30pm Fri-Sat. Full
service with take-out available.
Cash & credit cards & checks.
Mexican menu. Full bar.
Another good place to eat!

⑪ **CUCINA! CUCINA!** $$$
11am-11pm Mon-Thur, 11am-
12am Fri-Sat, 11am-10pm Sun.
Full service. Cash & credit
cards. Italian menu. Full bar.

⑫ **T.G.I.FRIDAY'S** $$
11am-11pm Sun-Thur, 11am-
12am Fri-Sat. Full service.
Cash & credit cards. American
menu. Full bar.

Fast Food

① **TACO BELL**
② **MCDONALD'S**
③ **BURGER KING**
⑥ **TACO TIME**
⑧ **LITTLE TOKYO TERIYAKI**
⑧ **LE DONUT**
⑦ **ARBY'S**
⑨ **HAPPY TERIYAKI**
⑩ **WENDY'S**

Other

④ **FIRESTONE** 7am-6pm
Mon-Fri, 8am-5pm Sat, noon-
5pm Sun. Cash & credit cards
& checks. Restrooms, phone.
Auto & tire repair shop.

⑧ **LINCOLN PLAZA**
  • Men's Wearhouse
  • Tower Books/Records
  • Big 5 Sporting Goods
  • General Cinemas
  • Mailboxes, Etc. (fax)

⑨ **RAINIER PLACE MALL**
  • Western Optical
  • Crown Books
  • Azteca
  • Red Robin
  • Happy Teriyaki
  • Abodio
  • Petco
  • Alphagraphics

⑬ **TACOMA MALL**
  • See Exit 130

Exit 133

This exit provides access to downtown Tacoma via Hwy 705, 38th Street via Hwy 7, and to the Tacoma Dome via 26th Street. The map below is for the Tacoma Dome-26th Street exit. Attractions at this exit include the Brown & Haley candy factory, the Tacoma Dome, and the Freighthouse Square Mall.

Key Features: Tacoma Dome, Freighthouse Square

Towing: Fife Towing 922-8784;   Gene's Towing 272-8633;
Herb's Towing 845-6750

Northbound: Southbound:

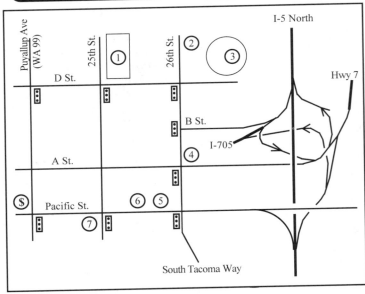

Service Stations

⑤ **TEXACO**   24 Hrs.
Self-serve, mini-mart, cash & credit cards, restrooms, ice, & phone.

Fast Food

⑦ **JACK IN THE BOX**

Lodging

② **RAMADA INN** ☺☺☺ $$$
(206) 572-7272 Non-smoking rooms & refrigerators available. Pets OK. Phone, cable TV, elevators, exercise area, & spa. Cash & credit cards & checks. Many discounts available. Covered parking, security doors to each floor, safe deposit boxes, & Budget Rent-A-Car available. *Attached restaurant:* MarSan Restaurant & Sports Bar, $$, American menu. Full bar.

Exit 133 *continued*

Other

① **FREIGHTHOUSE SQUARE**
- Antiques
- Small restaurants
- Speciality shops
- Craft & hobby shops
- Art galleries

③ **TACOMA DOME**

④ **BROWN & HALEY FACTORY OUTLET**
Home of Almond Roca candy!
Hours: 8:30am-5pm Mon-Fri, 10am-6pm Sat-Sun.

⑥ **ELEPHANT CAR WASH**

I-5, looking North from Exit 168A. Center set of Northbound lanes are the reversible Express Lanes.

Exit 134

You can reach the Tacoma Dome, Amtrak train station, and nearby Puyallup from this exit, along with 24-hour services. **This is a northbound exit only. See Exit 135 for map and details.**

Key Features: 24-hour gas, food, and lodging.

Towing:
Fife Towing 922-8784

Northbound exit only:

Exit 134

Portland Ave.

The Tacoma Dome, Exits 133, 134, & 135

Exit 135

The map below is for both Exits 134 and 135 in north Tacoma.
Key Features: Tacoma Dome, 24-hour gas, food, & lodging.
Towing: Fife Towing 922-8784; Turner Towing 627-0077

Northbound: Southbound:

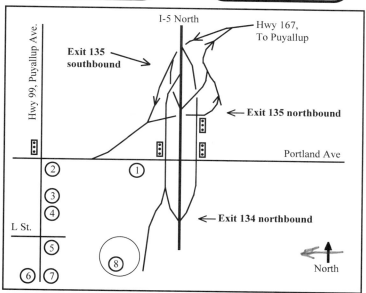

Service Stations

② ARCO AM/PM   24 Hrs.
Self-serve, mini-mart, cash & cash-machine cards, restroom, phone.

④ BP   24 Hrs.
Self-serve, mini-mart, cash & credit cards, diesel, phone, ice.

Fast Food

⑤ DAIRY QUEEN

Restaurants

③ PEGASUS $$
5am-9pm Mon-Sat, 6am-2pm Sun. Full and counter service. Cash & credit cards. American menu. Full bar.

⑦ MARILYN'S $$
24 Hrs. Full & counter service. Cash & credit cards. American menu. Full bar.

Lodging

① LA QUINTA INN ☺☺☺ $$
1-800-531-5900 Non-smoking rooms available. Elevators, cable TV, phone, refrigerators. Pets OK. Cash & credit cards & checks. Outdoor heated pool & spa. *Attached restaurant:* O'Callahan's, $$, American menu, full bar.

Other

⑥ AMTRAK TRAIN STATION
⑧ TACOMA DOME

Exit 136

Good food, lodging, gas, diesel, and easy access. Good exit for a rest stop!

Key Features: 24-hour gas and diesel, food, and lodging.

Towing: Fife Towing 922-8784

Northbound:

> ## Exit 136 A
> ### 20 St. E.

> ## Exit 136 B
> ### Port of Tacoma

Southbound:

> ## Exit 136
> ### Port of Tacoma

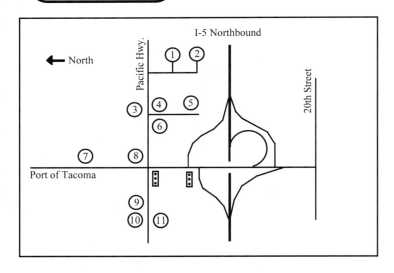

Service Stations

⑦ **FLYING J TRUCK PLAZA** 24 Hrs. Self-serve, large mini-mart, cash & credit cards, restrooms, phone, diesel. Professional trucker area with showers, outdoor picnic area, truck scales, propane. *Attached restaurant:* Thad's, $$

⑧ **TEXACO**　　　24 Hrs. Self-serve, large mini-mart, sit-down dining, cash & credit cards, diesel, drive-thru car wash, phone.

Restaurants

⑤ **LA CASA REAL**　　　$$ 11am-10pm Mon-Thur, 11am-11pm Fri-Sat, 10am-10pm Sun. (206) 922-8877 Full service with take-out available. Cash & credit cards & checks. Mexican menu. Full bar. Great food: worth a special stop.

Exit 136 *continued*

⑨ TURNING POINT $$
6am-9pm Mon-Sat, 8am-
8:30pm Sun. (206) 922-9555
Full service with take-out
available. Cash & credit cards
& checks. American menu. Full
bar.

Fast Food

⑥ JACK IN THE BOX

Lodging

① ECONO-LODGE   Reviewers
not permitted to see rooms. $$
(206) 922-0550   Non-smoking
rooms available. Wheelchair
access to 1st floor only. Cash &
credit cards & checks. Phone,
cable TV, outdoor seasonal pool.

② HOMETEL INN   ☺ $$
(206) 922-0555   Non-smoking
rooms available. Some rooms
have refrigerators & micro-
waves. Cash & credit cards.
Phones, cable TV, coin-op
laundry. Outdoor heated pool.
Attached restaurant: Jewel of
India, 10am-10pm daily, $$,
authentic Indian food. Cash &
credit cards.

③ GLACIER MOTEL   Reviewers
not permitted to see rooms. $$
(206) 922-5882   No handi-
capped access. Some rooms
with phones, refrigerators,
kitchenettes, & covered
parking. Cable TV.

⑩ DAYS INN   ☺☺ $$
1-800-274-9177   Non-smoking
rooms available. Some rooms
have refrigerators & kitchenettes. Cash & credit cards &
"not-local" checks. Free local
phone calls, cable TV. Pets OK.
Coin-op laundry, elevators.
Outdoor seasonal pool, video
movie rentals. Shuttle service to
Amtrack, Greyhound, & various
local truck or auto repair shops.
Local phone: 922-3500.

⑪ TRAVELERS INN   ☺ $$
(206) 922-9520   Non-smoking
rooms available. Some rooms
have refrigerators. Cash &
credit cards & checks. Senior
citizen and truck driver dis-
counts. Phones, cable TV.
Outdoor seasonal pool. Conti-
nental breakfast included.
Coffee in lobby.

Other

④ SAC'S DELI AND MINIMART

Exit 137

This exit features a number of very good restaurants, plenty of service stations and lodging, as well as several malls containing many other services. A visit to Camping World is a "must" for RV enthusiasts.

Key Features: 24-hour fuel, good restaurants, lodging, Camping World.

Towing: Fife Towing, 922-8784

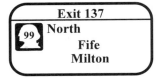

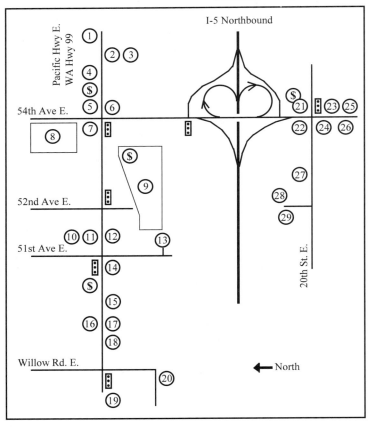

Service Stations

⑤ **BP** 24 Hrs.
922-9017 Self-serve, small mini-mart, cash & credit cards, restrooms, phone.

⑲ **ARCO AM/PM** 24 Hrs.
Self-serve, mini-mart, cash & credit cards, phone.

㉑ **TEXACO** 24 Hrs.
Self-serve, mini-mart, cash & credit cards, phone, handi-capped-access restrooms.

㉔ **BP** 24 Hrs.
Self- & full-serve, small mini-mart, cash & credit cards, phone, propane, RV pump-out.

Exit 137 *continued*

㉒ CHEVRON   24 Hrs.
Self-serve, mini-mart, cash & credit cards & checks, restrooms, phone.

㉗ ARCO AM/PM   24 Hrs.
Self-serve, small mini-mart, cash & credit cards.

Restaurants

③ CHRISTIE'S $$
(Located in the Executive Inn) 6am-11pm Mon-Sat, 6am-10pm Sun. (206) 922-0080 Full service with take-out available. Cash & credit cards. American menu. Full bar. Great food: worth a special stop.

⑥ MITZEL'S $$
6am-11pm Sun-Thur, 6am-12pm Fri-Sat. (206) 926-3144 Full service with take-out available. Cash & credit cards & checks. American menu. Beer & wine. Good food: pies & fresh turkey a speciality.

⑦ THE POODLE DOG $$
6am-2am Mon-Sat, 6am-12am Sun. (206) 922-6161 Full service, counter, & take-out available. Cash & credit cards & checks. American menu with full bar. Breakfast & lunch menu under $5. Very friendly.

⑯ KING'S PALACE $$
11am-10pm Mon-Fri, 11am-11pm Sat, 10am-9pm Sun. (206) 922-0911 Full service with buffet & take-out available. Cash & credit cards. American & Chinese menu. Full bar. Large salad bar & buffet.

⑱ PIZZA EXPERIENCE
$ 10:30am-11pm Sun-Thur, 10:30-midnight Fri-Sat. (206) 922-7337 Full service. Take-out & delivery available. Cash & credit cards. Italian menu featuring speciality pizzas. Beer. If you're in the mood for pizza, this is the place! It's worth a special stop.

㉘ JOHNNY'S AT FIFE $$
8am-12:30am Mon-Thur, 6am-1:30am Fri, 7am-1:30am Sat, 7am-10:30pm Sun. (206) 922-6686 Full service with take-out available. Cash & credit cards & checks. American menu. Full bar. Good food, gift shop.

Fast Food

⑨ **Baskin-Robbins**
⑨ **Denny's**
⑨ **Kentucky Fried Chicken**
⑫ WENDY'S
⑬ McDONALD'S
⑭ ARBY'S
⑮ SKIPPER'S
⑪ BURGER KING
㉖ BURGER BOX

Lodging

① ROYAL COACHMAN INN
1-800-422-3051 ☺☺☺ $$$
Non-smoking rooms available. Some rooms have recliners, kitchenettes, refrigerators. All rooms have coffee makers. Wheelchair access to 1st floor only. Cash & credit cards & checks. Local phone calls free, cable TV, indoor jacuzzi, gift shop in lobby. *Attached restaurant:* Castle Fife, $$, full service, good food.

Exit 137 *continued*

② Executive Inn ☺☺☺ $$$
1-800-938-8500 Non-smoking
rooms available. Elevators to
upper floors. Cash & credit
cards & checks. Phones, cable
TV. In-room coffee makers.
Indoor pool & spa with an
exercise area. Hertz car rental
available. *Attached restaurant:*
Christie's (reviewed separately)

④ Comfort Inn ☺ $$$
(206) 926-2301 Non-smoking
& handicapped rooms available.
Some rooms have kitchenettes
or spa. Cash & credit cards &
checks. Phone, cable TV.
Continental breakfast included.

⑩ King's Inn ☺ $$
(206) 922-3636 Non-smoking
rooms available. Kitchenette
with refrigerator available in
rooms rented by the week.
Wheelchair access. Cash &
credit cards. Phone, cable TV,
outdoor spa. Pets OK with fee.
Continental breakfast on
Sundays & free coffee in office.

㉙ Motel 6 Reviewers not
permitted to see rooms. $$
(206) 922-1270 Non-smoking
rooms available. Limited
wheelchair access. Cash &
credit cards. Cable TV, phone,
outdoor heated pool. One small
pet permitted per room.
Children under 17 free.

Other

⑧ Fife Square
• Better Foods
• Big Wheel Auto Parts
• Copy Wrights printing
• Laundromat

⑨ Fife Plaza
• Denny's (24 Hrs.)
• Kentucky Fried Chicken
• Ace hardware
• Valley Mart Pharmacy
• Shop-Rite supermarket
• Baskin-Robbins

⑰ Car Wash
Coin-op, for cars, trucks, & RVs.

⑳ Camping World 8am-5pm
7 days. RV "supermarket" with
a full line of parts & supplies.
They install everything they sell
(except Sundays). Cash &
credit cards, restrooms.

㉓ Fire Department

㉕ Fife Visitor Information
Center

Sea-Tac Rest Area

Northbound: At mile marker 140, this rest area provides the
following services:
- Phones
- RV Pump-out
- Vending Machines
- Free Coffee
- Restrooms

_____   _____
_____   _____
_____   _____
_____   _____
_____   _____
_____   _____
_____   _____
_____   _____
_____   _____

Truck Weigh Station

Southbound: At mile marker 141, this weigh station has phones.
No other services.

_____   _____
_____   _____
_____   _____
_____   _____
_____   _____
_____   _____
_____   _____

Exit 142

This exit features quick access to Auburn (via Hwy 18), Puyallup (via Hwy 161), Federal Way, & Fife (via Hwy 99).

Key Features: 24-hour gas, food, lodging, & hospital

Towing: Al's Towing 941-2888; Fife Towing 922-8784

Northbound:

| Exit 142A |
| **18** **East** **Auburn** **North Bend** |

| Exit 142B |
| **To** **99** **Federal Way** |

Southbound:

| Exit 142A |
| **18** **East** **Auburn** **North Bend** |

| Exit 142B |
| **161** **South** **Puyallup** **HOSPITAL** |

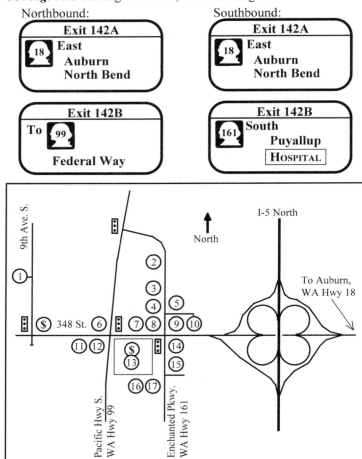

Service Stations

6 CHEVRON 24 Hrs.
Self-serve, mini-mart, cash & credit cards, restrooms, diesel, phone.

8 TEXACO 24 Hrs.
Self-serve, mini-mart, cash & credit cards, diesel, drive-thru car wash, handicapped access restooms, phone.

13 ARCO 24 Hrs.
Self-serve, large mini-mart, cash & credit cards, truck diesel, phone, propane. Handicapped-access restrooms, showers for truckers. Cash machine inside station. Part of Evergreen/Flying J Truck Stop. Truck washing available.

Exit 142 *continued*

Restaurants

⑰ PACIFIC HIGHWAY DINER
$$ 5am-11pm 7 days. Full &
counter service. Cash & credit
cards & checks. American
menu. Showers, laundromat,
TV room, video games, table
phones.

Fast Food

⑤ DAIRY QUEEN

⑦ McDONALD'S

⑨ DENNY'S

⑪ SUBWAY

⑫ BURGER KING

⑭ SHARI'S

⑮ POPEYE'S

Lodging

⑩ SUPER 8 ☺☺ $$$
1-800-800-8000 or (206) 838-8808
Non-smoking & handicapped
rooms available. One suite with
refrigerator. Wheelchair access
to 1st floor only. Cash & credit
cards & checks with VIP card.
Discounts with VIP card. Phone,
cable TV, guest laundry, coffee
in lobby. Pets OK with fee.
Plenty of truck parking.

⑯ ROADRUNNER ☺ $$
1-800-828-7202 or (206) 838-5763
Non-smoking rooms available.
Cash & credit cards &
commercial truck checks.
Phone, cable TV, guest laundry,
coffee & microwave in office.
Pets OK with fee.

Other

① ST. FRANCIS HOSPITAL

② GOODYEAR AUTO SERVICE
    CENTER

③ COOPER TIRES

④ TAYLOR RENTALS
    • Propane & kerosene

Exit 143

This exit provides access to Federal Way's main shopping areas: SeaTac Mall, SeaTac Village, and Gateway Center. There are so many good restaurants at this exit that it's hard to know where to start. You're sure to find something for everyone here!

Key Features: 24-hour gas, food, shopping, lodging. Numerous additional services along WA 99.

Towing:
Redondo Hts Wrecking 839-0280
Al's Towing 941-2888
Federal Way Towing 838-0426

```
Exit 143

Federal Way
So. 320th St.
```

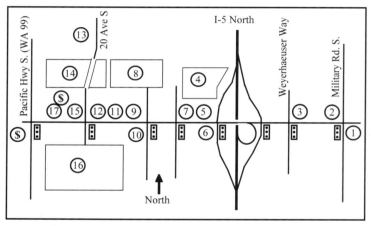

North

Service Stations

① **TEXACO**   24 Hrs.
Self-serve, mini-mart, phone, cash & credit cards. No restrooms.

② **ARCO AM/PM**   24 Hrs.
Self-serve, mini-mart, phone, cash & cash-machine cards. No restrooms.

⑥ **BP**   24 Hrs.
Self-serve, mini-mart, phone, cash & credit cards, drive-thru car wash. No restrooms.

⑨ **ARCO AM/PM**   5am-12am
Sat-Thur, 5am-1am Fri. Self-serve, phone, cash & cash-machine cards. No restrooms.

Restaurants

⑤ **BLACK ANGUS** $$
4pm-10pm Mon-Thur, 4pm-11pm Fri-Sat, noon-10pm Sun. Full service with take-out available. American menu, specializing in steak and prime rib. Full bar. Cash & credit cards. Cozy.

⑩ **RED ROBIN** $$
11am-2am 7 days. Sunday brunch 9am-2pm. Full service with take-out available. American menu specializing in meal-size burgers. Dining room has lots of atmosphere. Full bar. Cash & credit cards. Definitely worth a special stop!

Exit 143 *continued*

⑪ **RED LOBSTER** $$
11am-10pm Sun-Thur, 11am-11pm Fri-Sat. (206) 474-1262
Full service. Seafood menu.
Cash & credit cards & checks.
Full bar.

⑰ **BILLY McHALE'S** $$
11am-10pm Mon-Thur, 11am-11pm Fri, 11:30am-11pm Sat,
11:30am-10pm Sun. Full
service with take-out available.
American menu with lots of
variety. Dining room full of
"old-timey" relics. Full bar.
Cash & credit cards.

Fast Food

⑦ **McDONALD'S**
⑧ **WENDY'S**
⑧ **DENNY'S**
⑫ **TACO TIME**
⑭ **GODFATHER'S PIZZA**
⑮ **BURGER KING**

Lodging

⑬ **Best Western Execuutel**
☺☺☺ $$$ 1-800-528-1234,
local: 941-6000. Non-smoking
rooms available. Elevators to
upper floors, cable TV, phone,
refrigerator available. Indoor
pool and spa with complimen-
tary use of the Federal Way
Athletic Club next door. Cash
and credit cards. Discounts
available. Shuttle to Sea-Tac
airport & local restaurants.
Attached restaurant: Jimmy's,
$$, with full bar.

Other

③ **FIRE STATION**

④ **GATEWAY CENTER**
   10am-9pm
   • The Wherehouse Music
   • Gateway Cinemas
   • REI
   • TCBY Yogurt
   • Pier One Imports
   • Kinko's Copy Center
   • Many other shops

⑧ **CENTER PLAZA**
   • Best
   • See's Candy
   • Grand Peking Restaurant
   • Ichi Teriyaki
   • Bosley's Pet Food Mart
   • Ivar's Seafood
   • Godfather's Pizza
   • Denny's
   • Wendy's
   • Chinese Express
   • Many other shops

⑭ **SEA-TAC VILLAGE**
   9am-9pm
   • Big 5 Sporting Goods
   • Ernst Hardware
   • Payless Drugs
   • Crown Books
   • Many other shops

⑯ **SEA-TAC MALL** 10am-9pm
   Mon-Sat, 11am-6pm Sun
   • 21 fast-food restaurants
   • I.H.O.P.
   • Fresh Choice
   • Bon Marche
   • Lamont's
   • Sears
   • Mervyn's
   • Shoe Repair
   • One Hour Photomax
   • Many other shops

The concrete forest under Exit 164B.

Exit 147

This exit provides access (west) to Redondo, which features views of Puget Sound and a public beach. If you're hungry, be sure to stop at Rose's for an old-fashioned, home-style chicken dinner!

Key Features: Redondo, food and gas.

Towing: Redondo Heights Wrecking 839-0280

Exit 147

So. 272nd St.

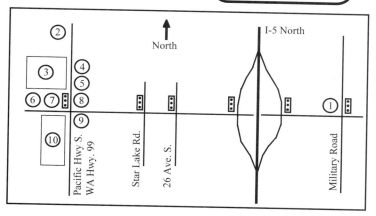

Service Stations

① **CIRCLE K**   24 Hrs.
Self-serve, mini-mart, restroom, phone, cash only.

⑨ **ARCO AM/PM**   24 Hrs.
Self-serve, mini-mart, restrooms, phone, cash & credit cards.

⑥ **TEXACO**   24 Hrs.
Self-serve, large mini-mart with eating area, restrooms, phone, cash & credit cards. Diesel, drive-thru car wash.

Restaurants

② **ROSE'S HIWAY INN** $$
4pm-9pm Tues-Fri, 12:30-9pm Sat, 12:30-8pm Sun, closed Mon. Full service with take-out available. American menu specializing in a home-style chicken dinner with all the trimmings. It's worth a special stop! Full bar. Cash & credit cards.

Fast Food

⑦ **JACK IN THE BOX**

③ **TACO BELL**

④ **SUBWAY**

Other

⑧ **WALT'S RADIATOR & MUFFLER**
• 8-6 M-F, 8:30-5 Sat
• 839-0666

⑤ **FIRESTONE AUTO SERVICE**
• 839-5670

③ **REDONDO SQUARE**
• Safeway (24 Hrs.)
• Taco Bell (24 Hrs.)
• Kiko Teriyaki
• Bartell Drugs
• Dolphin Pet
• Starbucks Coffee
• Many other stores

⑩ **LAUNDRY** - Coin-op.

Exit 149

This exit provides access to Highline Community College south on WA Hwy. 99, as well as various services.

Key Features:
Gas, food, & lodging

Towing:
Pete's Towing 878-8400 Dick's Towing 242-9901

Northbound:

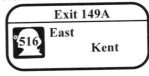

Southbound:

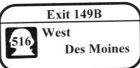

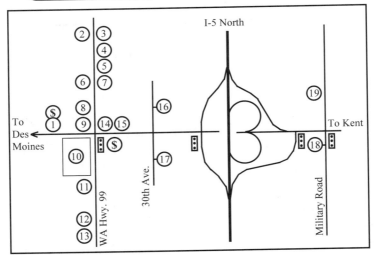

Service Stations

⑨ **TEXACO**   24 Hrs.
Self-serve, mini-mart, cash & credit cards, diesel, restrooms with handicapped access, phone.

⑪ **TEXACO**   24 Hrs.
Self-serve, mini-mart, cash & credit cards, restrooms, phone.

Restaurants

② **BK's KITCHEN** $$
6am-10pm 7 days. Full-service restaurant, counter or take-out available. American menu. Cash & credit cards & checks. Pies & baked goods available for take-out.

⑥ **BLOCKHOUSE** $$
11am-2am Mon-Sat, 12pm-2am Sun. Full-service restaurant. American menu. Cash & credit cards. Full bar.

Exit 149 *continued*

Fast Food

- ③ **McDonald's**
- ④ **Taco Bell**
- ⑧ **Meal Time Burger**
- ⑩ **Burger King**
- ⑩ **Pizza Hut**
- ⑫ **Baskin-Robbins**
- ⑬ **Skippers**
- ⑭ **Dunkin' Donuts**

Lodging

⑯ **King's Arms Motel** ☺ $$
(206) 824-0300 Cash & credit
cards. Weekly & monthly rates
& discounts available. Spacious
rooms. Non-smoking rooms
available. Some suites, some
rooms have kitchenettes, some
with refrigerators. Phones,
cable TV. Pets OK with fee.
Outdoor seasonal pool. Coffee
in the lobby.

⑰ **New Best Inn** ☺☺ $$
(206) 870-1280 Non-smoking
& handicapped rooms available.
Some rooms have kitchenettes.
Cash & credit cards. Discounts
& weekly rates available.
Phones, cable TV, including
HBO & Cinemax. Guest
laundry. No pets.

⑱ **Century Motel** ☺☺ $$
(206) 878-1840 Non-smoking
& handicapped rooms available.
Some rooms with kitchenettes,
some with refrigerators. Cash &
credit cards. Discounts &
weekly rates available. Phones,
cable TV. No pets.

Other

① **7-11**
- 24 Hrs.
- Cash machine
- Phone

⑤ **Midway Mail Center**
- Fax, Western Union

⑦ **Do-It-Yourself Car Wash**

⑩ **Midway Crossing**
- ~~QFC 24-Hours~~
- Burger King
- Pizza Hut
- Las Palomas Mexican Rest.
- Konich's Teriyaki
- Subway
- Phone
- Starbucks

⑮ **Midas Muffler**

⑲ **Valley I-5**
- RV Sales & Service
- 7:30am-5:30pm Mon-Fri
- Closed Sat & Sun
- Propane

Exit 151

This exit provides easy access to services, as well as Sea-Tac International Airport (north on International Blvd). There are numerous restaurants, service stations, and motels around the airport that can be reached from this exit.

Key Features: 24-hour gas, food, and lodging.

Towing: Pete's Towing 878-8400; Dick's Towing 242-9901; Airport Towing 243-6252

Exit 151

So. 200th St.
Military Rd.

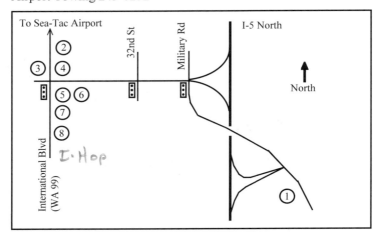

Service Stations

③ **CHEVRON** 24 Hrs.
Self- & full-serve, phone, cash & credit cards & checks, restrooms. Full service mechanic on duty 7am-7pm Mon-Fri, 9am-5pm Sat-Sun.

④ **BP** 24 Hrs.
Self-serve, mini-mart, phone, cash & credit cards, restrooms.

⑤ **7-11/ CITGO** 24 Hrs.
Self-serve, large mini-mart, phone, cash & credit cards, restrooms. Cash machine in store.

Restaurants

② **GIKAN #5 TERIYAKI** $$
11am-10pm Mon-Sat, 12pm-10pm Sun. 870-1500 Full service. Japanese menu. Full bar. Cash & credit cards.

Fast Food

⑦ **GODFATHER'S PIZZA**

Lodging

① **MOTEL 6** ☺☺ $$
(206) 824-9902. Non-smoking rooms available, cable TV, phone. Pets OK. Year-round outdoor heated pool and spa. Cash & credit cards. Handicapped rooms with roll-in showers for wheelchairs, oversized rooms, queen-size beds, & every room has a bathtub.

Other

⑥ **FIRE STATION**
⑧ **U-HAUL RENTAL CENTER**
   • Phone: 878-8158
   • Propane

Exit 152

This exit provides access to Sea-Tac International Airport (2 miles from the exit) as well as many nearby services. If you're camping, the South Seattle KOA Campground is also nearby. Additional services (not listed) along International Blvd.

Key Features: Sea-Tac International Airport

Towing: Pete's Towing 852-1050, Rebel's Towing 243-3630

Northbound:

> **Exit 152**
>
> **So. 188th St.**
> **Sea-Tac Airport**

Southbound:

> **Exit 152**
>
> **So. 188th St.**
> **Orillia Rd.**

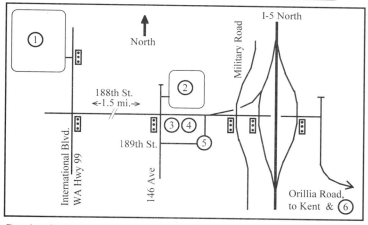

Service Stations

③ **BP**   24 Hrs.
Self-serve, mini-mart, phone, cash & credit cards, restrooms.

Restaurants

④ **OMNI** $$
5am-11pm Mon-Sat, 6am-9pm Sun. Full-service American menu, specializing in home-made pies. Counter service & take-out available. Beer & wine. Cash & credit cards & checks.

Lodging

⑤ **MOTEL 6**   Reviewers not permitted to see rooms. $$ (206) 241-1648. Handicapped & non-smoking rooms available. TV, phone, outdoor pool. Cash & credit cards.

Other

① **SEA-TAC INT'L AIRPORT**
② **VALLEY RIDGE PARK**
   • Tennis courts
   • Soccer and baseball fields
   • Community building
⑥ **SEATTLE SOUTH KOA CAMPGROUND**
   • (206) 872-8652
   • 5801 South 212th (two miles East, at light)

Exit 153

This exit features excellent hotels and shopping, *shopping*, *SHOPPING!* You are sure to find almost anything you need at Southcenter. This is a *Northbound* exit only. Use exit 154B to get to Southcenter from the North.

Key Features: Excellent hotels and SHOPPING!

Towing:
Dick's Towing 242-9901
Skyway Towing 226-8050

> **Exit 153**
>
> **Southcenter**
> **Parkway & Mall**

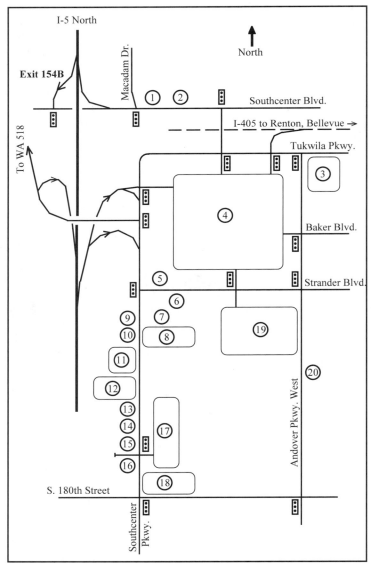

Service Stations

② ARCO AM/PM   24 Hrs.
Self-serve, mini-mart, cash &
credit cards & cash-machine
cards, restrooms, phone.

⑥ CHEVRON   24 Hrs.
Self- & full-serve, tiny mini-
mart, cash & credit cards, diesel,
restrooms with handicapped
access, phone. Mechanic on duty
7am-9pm Mon-Fri, 8am-6pm
Sat, 10am-6pm Sun.

Restaurants

⑭ TONY ROMA'S $$
11am-11pm Sun-Thurs, 11am-
12am Fri-Sat. Full service.
American menu specializing in
ribs. Cash & credit cards &
checks. Full bar.

⑮ WINNER'S $$$
11am-12:30am Mon-Tues,
11am-1am Wed-Thurs, 11am-
1:30am Fri-Sat, 9am-10pm Sun.
Full service. American menu.
Full bar. Cash & credit cards &
checks.

⑯ AZTECA $$
11am-10:30am Mon-Thurs,
11am-11:30pm Fri-Sat, 11am-
10pm Sun. Full service.
Mexican menu. Full bar. Cash
& credit cards & checks.

Fast Food

① DENNY'S
⑨ McDONALD'S
⑩ SIZZLER
⑬ WENDY'S

Lodging

⑤ DOUBLETREE INN   ☺☺☺
$$$ (206) 246-8220 Cash &
credit cards & checks. Handi-
capped & non-smoking rooms
available. Phones, cable TV.
Pets in carrier OK with fee.
Outdoor heated pool. Guests can
also use facilities at Doubletree
Suites. *Attached restaurant:*
Boojum Restaurant, $$$, full bar.

⑦ DOUBLETREE SUITES
☺☺☺ $$$$ (206) 575-8220
Cash & credit cards & checks.
Discounts available & frequent
flier credit available for some
airlines. All suites. Non-smoking
& handicapped suites available.
Phone, cable TV with a catalog
of available movies, elevators,
safe-deposit boxes, guest
laundry. Coffee in rooms, fresh-
baked cookies, breakfast, & free
drinks included. Pets OK with
fee. Indoor pool, spa, exercise
room, racketball courts. Shuttle
service to airport. *Attached
restaurant:* Peter B's, $$$.
Infinity Lounge. Hotel received
a Doubletree service award in
1993. Very helpful & friendly
staff.

⑳ MARRIOTT COURTYARD
☺☺☺ $$$ (206) 575-2500
Cash & credit cards & checks.
Discounts available. Suites
available. Non-smoking &
handicapped rooms available.
Interior courtyard rooms
available on request. Phone,
cable TV with HBO & ESPN,
elevators, guest laundry. No
pets. Coffee in lobby & in
room. Indoor pool, spa, exercise
room. Shuttle service to airport.
Attached restaurant: Courtyard
Cafe, $$, breakfast buffet.

Exit 153 *continued*

Other

③ **ANNEX AT SOUTHCENTER**
- Teriyaki Time
- Baseball World
- Seattle Lighting
- Pro Golf Discount
- Ballard Computer
- Many other stores
- Phone

④ **SOUTHCENTER MALL**
- Southcenter Theater
- Nordstrom
- The Bon Marche
- Sears
- Food Court
- JC Penney
- Ritz Diner
- Firestone Auto Center
- Mervyn's
- Many other shops & eating places, phones

⑧ **TOYS-R-US MALL**
- Toys-R-Us
- Godfather's Pizza
- China Coin Restaurant
- Miyabi Restaurant
- Magnolia Hi-Fi
- Phone
- Many other shops

⑪ **(NO NAME) MALL**
- Grazie Caffe Italiano
- Men's Wearhouse
- Car Toys
- La-Z-Boy
- Lamps Plus
- Many other shops

⑫ **CENTER PLACE MALL**
- Taco Time
- Subway
- Lucky Computer
- Hong Kong Express
- Mayflower of China
- Happy Teriyaki
- American Music
- Pier 1 Imports
- Phone
- Many other shops

⑰ **PARK WAY PLAZA**
- The Bon Home Store
- Azteca
- Act III Cinemas
- Red Robin
- Drug Emporium
- Cucina!Cucina!
- Ross
- Sportmart
- Egghead Software
- Video Only
- Silo
- Many other shops

⑱ **PAVILION MALL**
- Burlington Coat Factory
- Nordstrom Rack
- Marshall's
- Bergman Luggage
- Many other shops

⑲ **SOUTHCENTER PLAZA**
- Target
- Dahles' Big & Tall
- Zoopa Restaurant
- Burger King
- International Jewelers
- Sleep Country USA
- Silver Platters
- Starbucks Coffee
- Many other shops

Exit 154

Northbound, this exit leads either west to Burien or Renton via WA 518 or north on I-405, along the east side of Lake Washington.

Southbound, you have the same options. In addition, you can take this exit to Southcenter. See Exit 153 for a description of all the services available at Southcenter.

Key Features: Access to I-405, WA 518, and Southcenter Mall (fabulous shopping)

Towing:
Dick's Towing 242-9901
Skyway Towing 226-8050

Southbound *Left-hand* exit

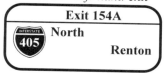

Northbound:

Southbound *Right-hand* exit

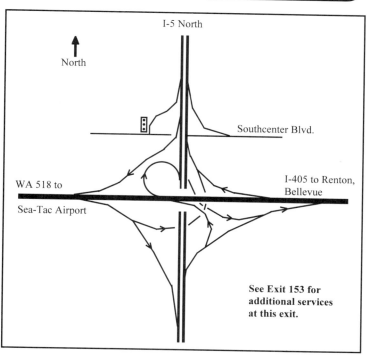

Exit 156

This exit provides easy on-off access to food, gas, and lodging.

Key Features: Food, gas, lodging

Towing: Dick's Towing 243-1647, Skyway Towing 226-8050

Northbound:

Southbound:

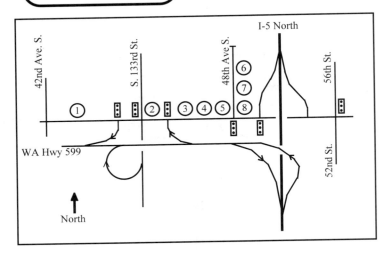

Service Stations

③ **UNOCAL 76**   24 Hrs.
Self- & full-serve, cash & credit cards, propane, restrooms, phone. Mechanic on duty 8:30-5:00 Mon-Sat.

⑤ **TEXACO**   24 Hrs.
Self- & full-serve, small mini-mart, cash & credit cards & checks, diesel, propane, restrooms with handicapped access, phone. Mechanic on duty 7-3 Mon-Fri.

⑧ **BP**   24 Hrs.
Self-serve, mini-mart, cash & credit cards, restrooms, phone. Mechanic 7-4:30 Mon-Fri.

Other

① **SUBURBAN PROPANE**
• 8-5 Mon-Fri, 8-12 Sat

Fast Food

② **TUKWILA DELI**

④ **JACK IN THE BOX**

⑦ **DENNY'S**

Lodging

⑥ **SILVER CLOUD INN** ☺☺ $$$
(800) 551-7207, (206) 246-0222
Cash & credit cards. Discounts available. Handicapped & non-smoking rooms available. Refrigerators, phones, cable TV with HBO, suites with microwave. No pets. Outdoor pool. Jacuzzi & exercise area. Coffee in the lobby. Continental breakfast. Copy machine available. Guest laundry. Plenty of truck parking.

Exit 157

This exit provides access to limited services Southbound only. See Exit 158 for additional services available nearby if Northbound.

Key Features: Gas

Towing: Dick's Towing 242-9901, Columbia Towing 722-2535

Northbound:

Exit 157
M. L. King Way

Southbound:

Exit 157
900 East
M. L. King Way

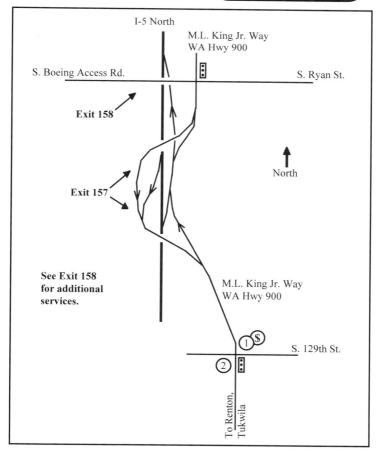

I-5 North

M.L. King Jr. Way
WA Hwy 900

S. Boeing Access Rd.   S. Ryan St.

Exit 158

North

Exit 157

See Exit 158
for additional
services.

M.L. King Jr. Way
WA Hwy 900

① $

②

S. 129th St.

To Renton, Tukwila

Service Stations

① **7-11 (CITGO)**   24 Hrs. Self-serve, large mini-mart, cash & credit cards, phone, cash machine.

② **BP**   5am-11pm, 7 days. Self-serve, mini-mart, cash & credit cards, diesel, phone, no restrooms. Mechanic on duty 8:30am-5pm Mon-Fri.

Exit 158

This exit provides access to Boeing Field (King County International Airport) and the Museum of Flight, as well as restaurants and accommodations. See Exits 157 & 161 for additional services.

Key Features: Boeing Field and the Museum of Flight

Towing: Dick's Towing 242-9901, Columbia Towing 722-2535

Northbound:

Exit 156
Airport Way **E. Marginal Way**

Southbound:

Exit 158
Pacific Hwy. S. **E. Marginal Way**

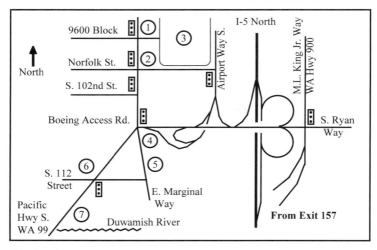

Service Stations

See Exit 157

Restaurants

② **RANDY'S** $$
24 Hrs. Full & counter service. American menu. Cash & credit cards. Airplanes everywhere.

Fast Food

⑤ **TUXEDO'S CAFE**
  • 9am-2pm Mon-Fri

Lodging

⑦ **HOLIDAY INN** ☺☺☺ $$$
(206) 762-0300   Cash & credit cards. Discounts & weekly rates available. Non-smoking & handicapped rooms available. Phones, cable TV with Showtime & Pay-per-View movies. Fax service available. Pets OK. Guest laundry. Outdoor heated pool. Coffee in lobby. Safe-deposit boxes. Shuttle service to airport. *Attached restaurant:* Lavender's Lounge (breakfast & dinner).

Other

① **MUSEUM OF FLIGHT**
③ **BOEING FIELD**
④ **CHECKER TOWING**
⑥ **PUGET SOUND TIRE**

Exit 161

This exit provides access to the north end of Boeing Field (King County International Airport). See Exits 158 and 162 for more services in the vicinity of Boeing Field.

Key Features: Boeing Field

Towing: Towmasters 682-4341, Columbia Towing 722-2535

Northbound:

Exit 161
Swift Ave. **Albro Place**

Southbound:

Exit 161
Albro Place **Swift Ave.**

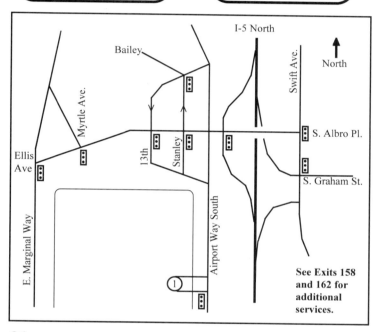

Other

① **KING COUNTY INT'L AIRPORT (BOEING FIELD)**
  • Terminal area has phone & restrooms

Exit 162

This is a *left-hand* exit going north. It provides access to food, gas, lodging, and alternate routes to downtown Seattle via E. Marginal Way, 4th Ave. South, and Airport Way South.

Key Features: Food, gas, lodging

Towing:
Dick's Towing 242-9901
GT Towing 938-4423

> **Exit 162**
>
> **Corson Ave.**
> **Michigan St.**

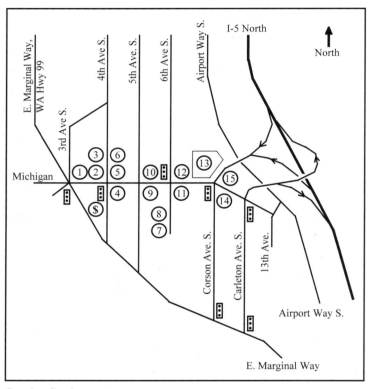

Service Stations

② **LIBERTY GAS** 7am-7pm Mon-Fri, 7am-4pm Sat, closed Sun. Mechanic on duty 8am-5pm Mon-Sat (Tayag's Auto Repair: 767-7008). Self-serve, tiny mini-mart, cash & credit cards, restrooms, phone.

⑨ **CHEVRON** 6am-8pm Mon-Fri, 7am-7pm Sat, closed Sun. Self- & full-serve, cash & credit cards & checks, restrooms with handicapped access, phone.

⑫ **TEXACO** 5:30am-11:30pm Mon-Fri, 7am-11:30pm Sat-Sun. Self-serve, large mini-mart, cash & credit cards, diesel, restrooms with handicapped access, phone.

⑭ **TEXACO** 24 Hrs. Self-serve, large mini-mart with deli, cash & credit cards, diesel, drive-thru car wash, restrooms with handicapped access, phone.

Exit 162 *continued*

Restaurants

⑥ **IKE'S** $$
10am-1am 7 days. Full and
counter service. American
menu. Cash & credit cards.

Fast Food

① **TACO TIME**

③ **McDONALD'S**

④ **POSEIDON FISH & CHIPS**

⑦ **KAUAI FAMILY RESTAURANT**

⑧ **THE WOKS DELI**

⑩ **BURGER KING**

⑪ **ARBY'S**

Lodging

⑤ **MAX-IVOR MOTEL** Reviewers
not permitted to see rooms. $$$
(206) 762-8194 Cash & credit
cards. Discounts available.
Some kitchenette units, some
refrigerators, phones, TV. No
pets. Guest laundry. Coffee in
office.

⑮ **GEORGETOWN INN** ☺☺
$$$ (206) 762-2233 Non-
smoking & handicapped rooms
available. Cash & credit cards.
Discounts available. Phones,
cable TV, elevators, guest
laundry. No pets. Weight room
& sauna. Coffee in lobby.

Other

⑬ **GEORGETOWN CENTER**
  • Daimonji Restaurant
  • Kim's Deli
  • Georgetown Bakery &
      Cafe
  • Amateur Radio Supply
  • Abodio
  • Woodcraft
  • Treasure House
  • Sony Service Center
  • Picture Source

Exit 163

This exit leads to the West Seattle Freeway, Puget Sound ferries, VA Hospital, and other services. Take the Spokane Street exit for ferries and services. Take Columbian Way for the VA Hospital.

Key Features: Ferries, VA Hospital, West Seattle Freeway

Towing:
Towmasters Towing 682-4341
Totem Towing 723-6595

Southbound:

Exit 163A
Spokane St.
Columbian Way

Northbound:

Exit 163
Spokane St.
Columbian Way

Exit 163B
6th Ave. S.
Forest St.

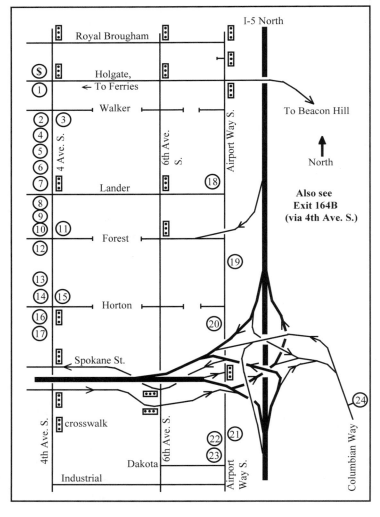

Exit 163 *continued*

Service Stations

③ **Arco am/pm**   24 Hrs.
Self-serve, large mini-mart,
cash & cash-machine cards, no
restrooms, phone.

⑦ **Texaco**   5am-10pm
Mon-Fri, 6am-8pm Sat, 9am-
7pm Sun. Self-serve, large
mini-mart, cash & credit cards,
diesel, phone, handicapped
restrooms.

⑭ **BP**   24 Hrs.
Self-serve, large mini-mart,
cash & credit cards, diesel,
truck scales, handicapped
restrooms, phone.

⑱ **Liberty Gas**   6am-5pm
Mon-Fri, 8am-5pm Sat., Closed
Sun. Self-serve, cash & credit
cards & checks, diesel, truck
scales, no restrooms.

Restaurants

⑬ **Andy's Diner** $$
6:30am-10:30pm Mon-Fri,
11:30-10:30 Sat, closed Sun.
Full service. American menu,
specializing in steak. Cash &
credit cards. Restaurant is
housed in old train dining cars.
Stairs to entrance. No ramp.

㉑ **Adolfo's** $$
11am-9:30pm Mon-Thurs,
11am-10pm Fri, 4:30pm-10pm
Sat, closed Sun. Full service.
Italian menu. Full bar. Cash &
credit cards.

Fast Food

① **Jack in the Box**
② **Taco Bell**
④ **McDonald's**
⑤ **Arby's**
⑨ **Subway**
⑪ **Denny's**
⑫ **By's Burgers**
⑯ **Burger King** (24 Hrs.)
⑰ **Yak's Deli**
⑳ **Elo's Philly Grill**
㉒ **Flynn's Cafe**
㉓ **Teriyaki Plus**

Other

⑥ **Postal Station Center**
  • Print King (copies, fax)
  • Deli-Mart
  • Westernco Donut
  • Phone
⑧ **Pyramid Tires**
⑩ **Elephant Car Wash**
⑮ **Fire Station**
⑲ **Rainier Brewery**
  • Tours 1pm-6pm Mon-Sat
㉔ **VA Hospital**

Exit 164

This exit provides access to Mercer Island, Bellevue, points east via Interstate 90, and downtown Seattle. Additional services are available at several nearby exits with easy access via 4th Avenue and Airport Way. See the map of downtown Seattle for services available at the James Street and Madison Street exits. Numerous Viet, Thai, and Chinese restaurants are located in the International District (the area between Dearborn and Jackson Streets).

Key Features: Downtown Seattle exits, Interstate 90, gas, & food
Towing: Columbia Towing 722-2535, Central Towing 323-3392

Northbound:

Exit 164A	
Dearborn St. **James St.** **Madison St.** **INTERSTATE 90 East**	
Hospital	**Spokane**

Southbound:

Exit 164	
INTERSTATE 90 East **Dearborn St.** **Airport Way**	
Spokane	

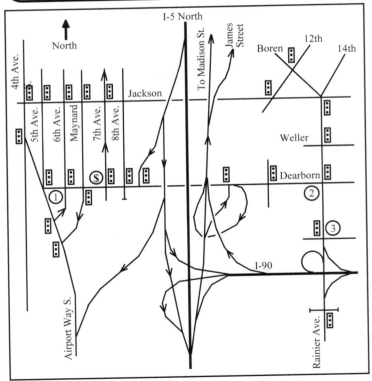

Service Stations

① **TEXACO**   24 Hrs.
Self-serve, large mini-mart, cash & credit cards, ice, phone.

③ **TEXACO**   24 Hrs.
Self-serve, large mini-mart, cash & credit cards, restrooms, phone. Drive-thru car wash.

Other

② **RAINIER VETERINARY HOSPITAL**

Exit 164B

This is a *Northbound* exit only, convenient to the Seattle Kingdome, ferry terminal, and Amtrak train station. There are numerous restaurants and hotel facilities in the immediate vicinity, especially as you proceed downtown, to the north. There are also connections to other freeway exits in the vicinity, especially along 1st Avenue and 4th Avenue. See Exit 163 for additional services and the map of downtown Seattle for nearby attractions.

Key Features: Kingdome, Amtrak, Puget Sound ferries, downtown Seattle

Towing:
Pete's Towing 878-8400
Lincoln Towing 622-0415
Day & Night Towing 633-0415

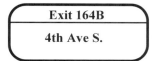

Exit 164B

4th Ave S.

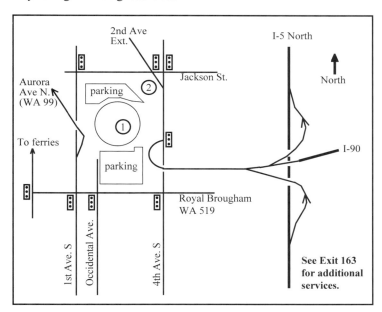

Other

(1) **KINGDOME**
  • Ample parking on Royal Brougham and Jackson Streets.

(2) **AMTRAK TRAIN STATION**
  • Look for the clock tower.

Downtown Seattle

The map of downtown Seattle on the facing page shows the entrances and exits in the downtown core of the city, as well as tourist highlights. There are numerous restaurants and hotels throughout the downtown area, but parking is limited to on-street meters, garages, and pay-by-the-hour lots.

Service Stations

(10) **CHEVRON** 24 Hrs. Self- & full-serve, mini-mart, cash & credit cards, restrooms. Mechanic on duty 7am-3:30pm Mon-Fri.

Other

(1) **SEATTLE CENTER**
- Space Needle Restaurant
- Coliseum & Arena
- Opera House
- Center House
- Pacific Science Center
- Children's Museum
- Numerous other restaurants, picnic areas

(2) **SEATTLE AQUARIUM**

(3) **PIKE STREET MARKET**
- Restaurants, shops
- Farmer's market

(4) **WESTLAKE CENTER**
- Multi-level mall
- Shops, restaurants
- Monorail boarding for a ride to Seattle Center (every 15 minutes)

(5) **SEATTLE ART MUSEUM**

(6) **WASHINGTON STATE CONVENTION AND TRADE CENTER**

(7) **VIRGINIA MASON MEDICAL CENTER**

(8) **WASHINGTON STATE FERRIES**
- Bremerton and Winslow
- Approach from the South if taking your car onto the ferry.

(9) **PIONEER SQUARE**
- Numerous restaurants
- Underground Tour
- Antique shops
- Art galleries

(11) **SWEDISH HOSPITAL**

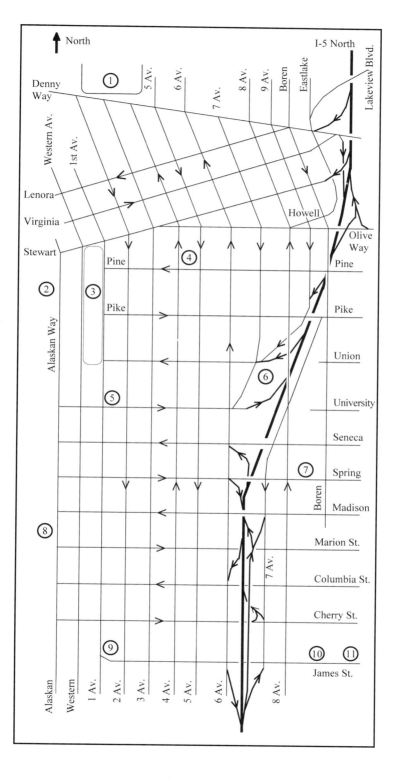

Exit 165

The *express lanes* to by-pass most of downtown & north Seattle traffic begin just prior to this exit when headed *Northbound.*

Key Features: Seattle's theater district, hotels & restaurants.

Towing: Day & Night Towing 633-0415; Pete's Towing 878-8400

Northbound:

Exit 165
Seneca St.

Southbound:

Exit 165A
James St.

Exit 165B
Union St.

Please refer to the map of downtown Seattle for the general services and attractions available at the downtown exits.

Exit 166

This exit provides easy access to Seattle's Capital Hill district via Olive Way and to the Seattle waterfront and Seattle Center via Stewart and Denny.

Key Features: Capital Hill & the north end of downtown Seattle.

Towing: Lincoln Towing 622-0415; Columbia Towing 722-2535

Northbound:

Exit 166
Olive Way

Southbound:

Exit 166
Stewart St. **Denny Way**

Please refer to the map of downtown Seattle for the general services and attractions available at the downtown exits.

Exit 167

This exit features fine dining on Lake Union's waterfront and easy access to the Seattle Center.

Key Features: Lake Union and the Seattle Center.

Towing: Lang Towing 322-3383
Lincoln Towing 622-0415

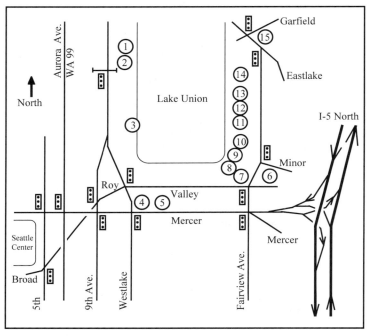

Service Stations

④ **UNOCAL 76**   24 Hrs.
Full- and self-serve, cash & credit cards, diesel, restrooms, phones. Mechanic available 8am-5pm Mon-Fri. 923-8272.

Restaurants

① **LATITUDE 47** $$$
Lunch: 11am-4pm Mon-Fri, Dinner: 5pm-9:30pm 7 days. Sun. Brunch: 10am-2:30pm. 284-1047. Full service. Cash & credit cards. American menu specializing in seafood. Full bar. On Lake Union.

② **KAYAK GRILL** $$
Lunch: 11:15pm-2:30pm Mon-Fri. Dinner: 5pm-10pm Mon-Thurs, 5pm-10:30pm Fri-Sat, closed Sun. Full service. Cash & credit cards. Steak & seafood. Full bar. Patio dining on the water.

⑧ **BENJAMIN'S** $$
Lunch: 11:30am-2pm Mon-Fri, 10:30am-2pm Sun. Dinner: 4:30pm-10pm 7 days. 621-8262. Full service. Cash & credit cards & checks. Chicken, seafood, & pasta. Full bar. Outdoor deck overlooking Lake Union.

Exit 167 *continued*

⑩ **CUCINA! CUCINA!** $$
11:30pm-11pm Mon-Thur,
11:30am-12pm Fri-Sat,
11:30am-10pm Sun. 447-2782.
Full service. Cash & credit
cards. Italian menu. Full bar.
On Lake Union.

⑪ **T.G.I.FRIDAY'S** $$
11am-2am Mon-Sat, 10am-2am
Sun. Full service. 621-7290.
Cash & credit cards & checks.
American menu. Full bar. On
the water.

⑬ **DUKE'S** $$$
Bkfst: 6:30am-10am Mon-Fri,
8am-2pm Sat-Sun, Lunch:
11am-4pm 7 days. Dinner:
4pm-10pm Sun-Thurs, 4pm-
11pm Fri-Sat, closed Sun.
292-9402. Full service. Cash &
credit cards. Seafood menu.
Full bar. Outdoor dining on the
water.

⑭ **KAMON** $$$
Lunch: 11:30pm-2:30pm Mon-
Fri. Dinner: 5pm-10pm Sun-
Thurs, 5pm-11pm Fri-Sat.
622-4665. Full service. Cash &
credit cards & checks. Japanese
menu. Full bar. Outside deck
overlooking Lake Union.

Fast Food

⑤ **DENNY'S**

⑦ **BURGER KING**

⑧ **BENJI'S FISH & CHIPS**

⑫ **QUICK FIX JUICE & JAVA BAR**

Lodging

⑥ **RESIDENCE INN** ☺☺☺ $$$$
624-6000 or 1-800-331-3131.
Cash & credit cards & checks.
Non-smoking & handicapped
rooms available. All suites,
with kitchenettes, phones, cable
TV, balconies. Pets OK with
fee. Indoor heated pool, spa,
steam room, sauna, large
exercise area. Fax, copy
machine, guest laundry, & safe-
deposit boxes available.
Complimentary shuttle service,
shopping service, and dessert
in the evening. Continental
breakfast served in large central
atrium.

Other

③ **KENMORE AIR TERMINAL**
(Seaplane terminal)
(206) 486-1257

⑨ **CHANDLER'S COVE**
• Retail shops
• Chandler's Crabhouse
• Duke's Chowder House

⑫ **YALE STREET LANDING**
• (same building as
  T.G.I.Friday's)
• I Love Sushi
• Opus Too Grill

⑮ **EASTLAKE VETERINARY
    HOSPITAL**

Exit 168A

This exit is primarily a residential area with only a few services.

Key Features: Food, lodging

Towing: Lincoln Towing 622-0415

Northbound:

> **Exit 168A**
>
> **Lakeview Blvd.**

Southbound:

> **Exit 168A**
>
> **Boylston Ave.**
> **Roanoke St.**

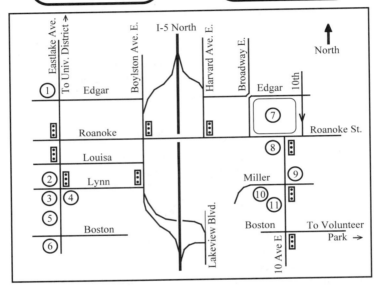

Restaurants

③ **THAN YING THAI CUISINE** $$
11:30am-10pm Mon-Fri, 5pm-
10pm Sat-Sun. Full service. Cash &
credit cards. Full bar.

⑥ **SERAFINA'S** $$
Lunch: 11:30pm-2:30pm Mon-Fri.
Dinner: 5:30pm-10pm Sun-Thurs,
5:30pm-11pm Fri-Sat. Full service.
Cash & credit cards. Italian menu.
Full bar. Patio dining in good
weather. Diners over 21, only.

⑩ **GALERIA'S** $$
11am-10pm Mon-Thur, 11am-
11pm Fri, noon-11pm Sat, 4pm-
10pm Sun. Full service. Cash &
credit cards. Mexican menu. Full
bar.

Fast Food

① **DALY'S DRIVE IN**
② **PAZZO'S PIZZA**
④ **SUBWAY, YUMIKO TERIYAKI**
⑨ **PAGLIACCI PIZZA**
⑪ **DOMINO'S PIZZA**

Lodging

⑤ **EASTLAKE INN** ☺ $$$
(206) 322-7726 Cash & credit
cards. Discounts available. Non-
smoking rooms available. All
rooms have kitchenettes, phones,
cable TV. Fax available.

Other

⑦ **ROANOKE PARK**
  • Children's play area
⑧ **FIRE STATION**

Exit 168B

This exit provides access to WA 520, going east across Lake Washington to Bellevue, Kirkland, and I-405. Left-hand exit *southbound*.

Key Features: WA 520 East to Bellevue and Kirkland

Towing: Lincoln Towing 622-0415

Northbound: Southbound: *Left-hand* exit

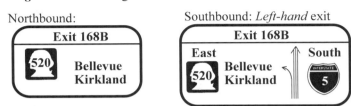

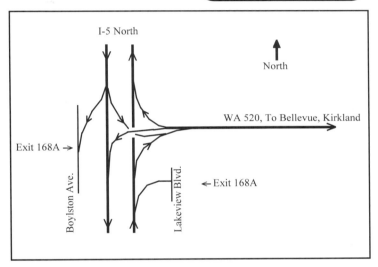

No Services

Exit 169

This exit provides access to the University of Washington (East on 45th) and the Woodland Park Zoo (several miles West on 45th). There are numerous restaurants along University Way that are not shown due to a lack of off-street parking in the area.

Key Features: University of Washington & Woodland Park Zoo.

Towing: Lang Towing 322-3383; AM/PM Towing 365-0330

Northbound:

Exit 169
N.E. 45th St. **N.E. 50th St.**

Southbound:

Exit 169
N.E. 50th St. **N.E. 45th St.**

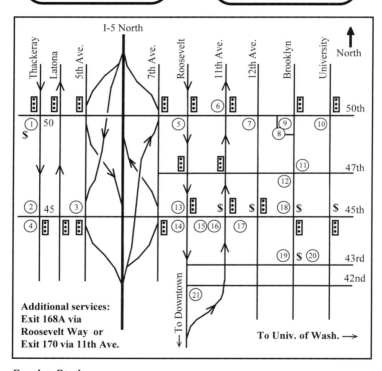

Service Stations

① **7-11 CITGO**   24 Hrs.
Self-serve, large mini-mart with indoor seating area, cash & credit cards, restrooms, phone. Cash-machine in store.

② **TEXACO**   24 Hrs.
Self-serve, mini-mart, cash & credit cards, diesel, handi-capped-access restrooms, phone.

Exit 169 *continued*

⑪ CHEVRON   24 Hrs.
Self-serve, large mini-mart, cash & credit cards, handicapped-access restrooms, phone, ice.

⑫ BP   24 Hrs.
Self-serve, mini-mart, cash & credit cards, phone, ice, no restrooms.

⑭ UNOCAL 76   24 Hrs.
Full- & self-serve, cash & credit cards, restrooms, phone, ice. Mechanic available 7am-5pm Mon-Fri, 10am-5pm Sat-Sun.

⑯ TEXACO   24 Hrs.
Self-serve, large mini-mart, cash & credit cards, handicapped-access restrooms, phone.

Restaurants

⑤ INDIA HOUSE $$
5pm-12am 7 days. Full service. Cash & credit cards. Indian menu. Full bar.

⑨ CEDARS $$
11am-10:30pm Mon-Thurs, 11am-11pm Fri-Sat, 9am-10:30pm Sun. 527-5247 Full service with take-out available. Cash & credit cards & checks. Middle Eastern & Indian menu. Beer.

⑬ THE KEG $$
11am-11pm Mon-Fri, 4pm-11pm Sat-Sun. Full service. Seafood & steak menu. Full bar. Cash & credit cards & checks.

⑰ CHINA FIRST $$
11am-10pm 7 days. 633-1538 Full service with take-out available. Cash & credit cards. Chinese menu.

⑳ RISTORANTE TOSCANA $$$
5pm-11pm Wed-Mon, closed Tues. 547-7679 Full service. Cash & credit cards. Full bar. Limited handicapped access. Excellent Italian dining.

Fast Food

① WINCHELL'S DONUT HOUSE
⑥ IVAR'S
⑧ BURGER KING
⑨ JACK IN THE BOX
⑭ SUBWAY (24 HRS)
⑭ WESTERNCO DONUT
    (24 HRS)
⑭ BASKIN-ROBBINS
⑭ BBQ ON A BUN
⑭ TERIYAKI PLUS
⑱ INTERNATIONAL HOUSE OF
    PANCAKES (24 HRS)

Lodging

③ UNIVERSITY PLAZA ☺☺
$$$ 634-0100 or 1-800-343-7040 Non-smoking & handicapped rooms available. Refrigerators available by request. Some suites available. Cash & credit cards & checks. Discounts available. Phones, cable TV, outdoor seasonal pool, exercise area, elevators, beauty shop. No pets. Meeting rooms, fax, & valet laundry service. *Attached Restaurant:* Excalibur's, $$$, full bar, live entertainment in lounge.

Exit 169 *continued*

(18) **MEANY TOWER** ☺☺☺ $$$
634-2000 or 1-800-648-6440
Non-smoking & handicapped
rooms available. Cash & credit
cards & checks. Discounts
available. Phones, exercise
area, elevators, safe-deposit
boxes. No pets. Meeting rooms,
fax, & valet laundry service.
Easy walk to U. of Washington.
Restaurant: Meany Tower Grill,
$$, full bar.

(21) **UNIVERSITY INN** ☺☺☺
$$$ 545-1504 or 1-800-733-
3855 Non-smoking & handi-
capped rooms available. Some
rooms have kitchenettes, suites
available. Cash & credit cards
& checks. Discounts available
& kids stay free in parents'
room. Phones, cable TV, spa,
outdoor pool, & exercise area,
elevators, safe-deposit boxes.
No pets. Fax. Coin-op & valet
laundry. Easy walk to Univ. of
Washington. Continental
breakfast, coffee in lobby 24
Hrs. Good stop for families.
Very friendly. Hotel recently
expanded & remodeled.

Exit 170

This is a *Northbound* exit only. It leads to a congested residential area with many small shops and services. It is close to Green Lake and the north end of the University District.

Key Features: Green Lake, the University District

Towing:
Lincoln Towing 622-0415
Day & Nite Towing 633-5400

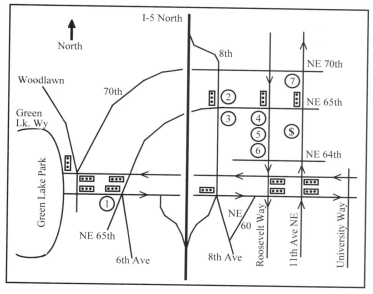

Service Stations

② **TEXACO**   24 Hrs.
Self-serve, mini-mart, cash & credit cards, diesel, drive-thru car wash, restrooms with handicapped access, phone.

③ **ARCO AM/PM**   24 Hrs.
Self-serve, mini-mart, cash & cash machine cards, restrooms, phones.

Restaurants

④ **HIMALAYA** $$
Lunch: 11:30am-2:30pm Mon-Sat, 12pm-2:30pm Sun. Dinner: 5pm-10:00pm Sun-Thurs, 5pm-11pm Fri-Sat. Full service Indian menu. Beer. Cash & credit cards.

⑤ **WANZA** $$
Lunch: 11:30am-2:30pm Tues-Sat. Dinner: 5pm-9pm Tues-Thurs, 5pm-10pm Sat-Sun. Closed Mon. Full service. Cash & credit cards. Ethiopian menu.

⑥ **SUNLIGHT CAFE** $$
11am-9pm Mon-Fri, 10am-9pm Sat-Sun. Full & counter service. Cash & credit cards. Vegetarian menu & espresso.

Fast Food

① **BOEHM CANDY KITCHEN**

Other

⑦ **QFC** (24-Hrs., Phone)

Exit 171

This exit provides access to Green Lake on the west and Lake City Way on the east. In addition to the services listed here, there are many additional services around Green Lake, as well as farther east on Lake City Way. Also see Exits 173 (north) and 169 & 170 (south).

Key Features: Green Lake, Lake City Way

Towing: Road Runner 367-0151; Lincoln Towing 622-0415

Northbound:

> ## Exit 171
> **522** **Bothell**
> **Lake City Wy.**

Southbound:

> ## Exit 171
> **N.E. 71st St.**
> **N.E. 65th St.**

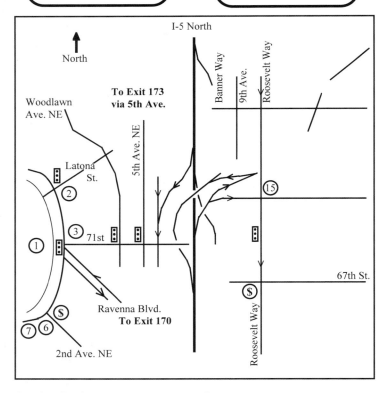

Service Stations

⑭ **BP** 24 Hrs.
Self-serve, tiny mini-mart, cash & credit cards, ice, restrooms, and phone. Mechanic on duty 8am-5pm Mon-Fri. AAA emergency service.

Restaurants

② **RASA MALAYSIA** $$
5pm-10pm Sun-Thurs, 5pm-11pm Fri-Sat, Lunch daily 11:30am-2:30pm. Full service with take-out available. Cash & credit cards. Vegetarian menu featuring noodles, curry, juices.

Exit 171 *continued*

④ **CHINA CITY** $$
11am-9pm Mon-Thurs, 11am-10pm Fri, noon-10pm Sat. Cash & credit cards. Full service. Chinese menu.

⑧ **GASPARE'S RISTORANTE ITALIANO** $$$
5pm-10pm Tues-Thurs & Sun, 5pm-10:30pm Fri-Sat, closed Mon. Non-smoking restaurant. No reservations. Cash & credit cards. Full service. Italian menu. Wine available.

⑨ **KING'S CHINESE** $$
11:30am-10pm Tues-Thurs, 11:30am-11pm Fri, 4pm-10pm Sat-Sun. Full service. Chinese & Thai menu featuring natural ingredients, brown & white rice, no msg.

⑩ **COOPER'S NW ALE HOUSE** $$
Dinner every day, lunch on weekends. Cash & credit cards. Burgers, fish & chips. Many micro-brews available.

⑬ **NEW PEKING** $$
4pm-10pm Mon-Thur, 4pm-11pm Fri-Sun, Lunch 11:30am-2:30pm Mon-Fri. (206)523-1010 Full service with take-out available. Cash & credit cards & checks. Chinese menu. Full bar.

⑯ **LUNA-ROSSA** $$
5pm-10pm Tue-Sun, closed Mon. 527-4778 Full service. Cash & credit cards & checks. Italian menu. Beer & wine.

Fast Food

③ **BASKIN-ROBBINS**

⑤ **SPUD FISH & CHIPS**

⑥ **HAAGEN DAZS**

⑦ **THE FRANKFURTER**

⑫ **PIZZA TIME**

Other

① **GREEN LAKE PARK**
- Picnic area
- Tennis
- Children's play area
- Boat rentals
- Restrooms
- Phones
- Swimming
- Fishing tackle rentals
- Sailboard rentals
- Jogging and bicycle paths
- Sports fields

⑪ **ALL THE BEST PET CARE**

⑮ **SAFEWAY** (24 HRS.)

Exit 172

This exit leads to a mostly residential area. However, there are many restaurants, motels, and other services along Aurora Ave, WA Hwy 99.

Key Features: Gas

Towing: City Towing 283-0860, Day & Nite Towing 633-5400

Northbound:

Exit 172
N. 85th St. Aurora Ave. N.

Southbound:

Exit 172
N. 85th St. N.E. 80th St.

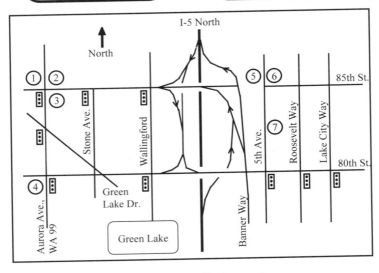

Service Stations

① **ARCO AM/PM**   24 Hrs.
Self-serve, mini-mart, cash & cash machine cards, no restrooms, phone.

③ **BP**   24 Hrs.
Self-serve, diesel, cash & credit cards, restrooms, phones, espresso.

⑥ **CHEVRON**   7am-9pm
Mon-Fri, 6am-8pm Sat. Self- & full-serve, tire service, cash & credit cards, restrooms. Mechanic 8am-5pm Mon-Sat.

Restaurants

⑤ **THE BELLS** $$
11am-8pm Mon-Sat, noon-8pm Sun. Full service. Cash, credit cards, & checks. American menu with home-made pies. Limited off-street parking.

Fast Food

② **JACK IN THE BOX**
⑦ **ALEKO'S PIZZA**

Other

④ **ANDY'S AUTO REPAIR**
• 784-4727

Gazebo built over a giant tree stump,
Chehalis Recreational Park, Exit 76.

Exit 173

The Southbound *express lanes* (left-hand exit) start at this exit. They allow you to bypass some of the local Seattle traffic, if you are travelling through. If you need a stop or are coming to Seattle to shop, this exit has shopping galore and several great places to eat, as well as a motel and other services.

Key Features: Northgate Mall

Towing:
Northgate Towing 364-1500
Lang Towing 322-3383

```
Exit 173

Northgate Wy.
1st Ave. N.E.
```

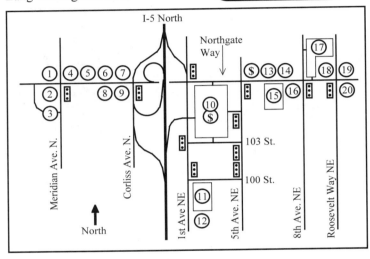

Service Stations

(2) **TEXACO**   24 Hrs.
Self-serve, mini-mart, cash & credit cards, diesel, restrooms with handicapped access, phone.

(7) **CHEVRON**   24 Hrs.
Self- & full-serve, tiny mini-mart, cash & credit cards, good restrooms with handicapped access, phones. Mechanic on duty 8am-6pm Mon-Fri, minor repairs 8am-8pm Sat, 10am-7pm Sun.

(8) **BP**   24 Hrs.
Self- & full-serve, large mini-mart, propane, cash & credit cards, phone, no restrooms. Mechanic available for major & minor repairs 9am-5pm Mon-Sat. Phone: 367-9006.

(18) **BP**   7am-12am, 7 days.
Self-serve, mini-mart, cash & credit cards, phone, restrooms. Full-service mechanic on duty 7am-5pm Mon-Sat.

(20) **ARCO AM/PM**   24 Hrs.
Self-serve, mini-mart, cash & cash machine cards, no restrooms, phone.

Restaurants

(1) **BARNABY'S** $$
Lunch: 11:30am-2pm Mon-Fri. Dinner: Starts at 5pm Mon-Sat, 4pm Sun. Full service. Cash & credit cards. American menu specializing in steak & seafood. Full bar. "Old English" atmosphere.

Exit 173 *continued*

⑫ **MARIE CALLENDER'S** $$
8am-10pm Mon-Thurs, 8am-11pm Fri, 9am-11pm Sat, 9am-10pm Sun. Full service & counter. Cash & credit cards. American menu. Good food & great pies.

Fast Food

③ **ARBY'S**
⑤ **DENNY'S**
⑨ **MCDONALD'S**
⑬ **STARBUCKS COFFEE**
⑭ **SIZZLER**
⑯ **PANCAKE HAUS**
⑲ **SKIPPER'S**

Lodging

⑥ **RAMADA INN**   ☺☺☺ $$$
365-0700 Non-smoking & handicapped rooms available. Some rooms have kitchenettes, including dishes & flatware. Some suites available. Cash & credit cards & checks. Phones, cable TV, outdoor seasonal pool, elevators, gift shop in lobby. Crib & roll-aways free. Small pets OK. Complimentary van to U. of Washington hospitals & downtown areas. Passes to Seattle Athletic Club available. Room service available from nearby Denny's Restaurant. Food discount of 10% available from nearby Barnaby's Restaurant with room key. VCR rentals available. Coffee in lobby.

Other

④ **7-11 MALL**
  • 7-11
  • Teriyaki Plus
  • Sudden Printing
  • Family Donut
  • Rose Garden Florist
  • Phone

⑩ **NORTHGATE MALL**
  • 9:30am-9:30pm Mon-Sat, 11am-6pm Sun
  • JC Penney
  • Nordstrom
  • Bon Marche
  • Lamont's
  • Ernst
  • QFC supermarket
  • Red Robin
  • Cinemas
  • Cash machine
  • Phones
  • Many other shops
  • Many places to eat

⑪ **NORTHGATE STATION MALL**
  • Round Table Pizza
  • Sub Shop
  • Lazerquick
  • SAS Shoes
  • Mailboxes, etc.
  • Silver Platters
  • Phone

⑮ **NORTHGATE PLACE MALL**
  • Taco Time
  • Thai Hut Restaurant
  • Sir Speedy Printer
  • Tony Roma's
  • Azteca
  • Countryside Donut House

⑰ **NORTHGATE VILLAGE MALL**
  • Kinko's Copies
  • Drug Emporium
  • TJ Maxx
  • Baskin-Robbins
  • Shoe Pavilion
  • North China Restaurant
  • The Frankfurter
  • Others

Exit 174

This is a *Northbound* exit only. It provides access to food, gas, and other local services.

Key Features: Food, gas

Towing:
Shannon Towing 774-8811
Lang Towing 322-3383

> **Exit 174**
>
> **N.E. 130th St.**
> **Roosevelt Way**

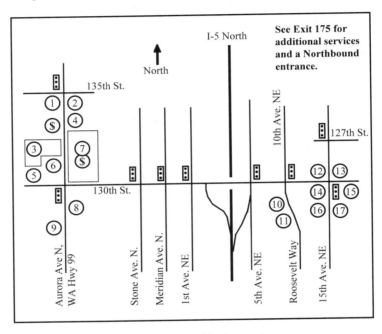

I-5 North

See Exit 175 for additional services and a Northbound entrance.

North

135th St.

127th St.

130th St.

10th Ave. NE

Aurora Ave N,
WA Hwy 99

Stone Ave. N.

Meridian Ave. N.

1st Ave. NE

5th Ave. NE

Roosevelt Way

15th Ave. NE

Service Stations

① **ARCO**   6am-9pm
Mon-Fri, 8am-8pm Sat-Sun.
Self-serve, cash, restrooms,
phone. Behind Arco is Lee's
Auto Repair, 362-4449.

⑫ **CHEVRON**   24 Hrs.
Self- & full-serve, mini-mart,
propane, cash & credit cards,
restrooms, phones. AAA-
approved auto repair: 8am-5pm
Mon-Fri, 8am-3pm Sat.

⑭ **7-11 (CITGO)**   24 Hrs.
Self-serve, large mini-mart,
cash & credit cards, phone, ice,
cash machine. No restrooms.

Restaurants

⑤ **ASIAN PALACE** $$
11am-11pm 7 days. Full service
with take-out available. Cash &
credit cards. Korean, Chinese,
and sushi menu. Full bar.

⑥ **INDIA PALACE** $$
11am-10pm 7 days. Buffet with
take-out available. Cash & credit
cards. Indian menu. Beer
available.

⑧ **LITTLE BEIJING** $$
11am-10pm Tues-Sun, closed
Mon. Full service with take-out
available. Cash & credit cards.
Chinese menu.

Exit 174 *continued*

⑪ **GOURMET CITY** $$
11:30am-10pm Sun-Thurs,
11:30am-10:30pm Fri-Sat.
365-8288 Full service with
take-out available. Cash &
credit cards. Chinese menu.
Full bar.

Fast Food

② **KENTUCKY FRIED CHICKEN**
④ **IVAR'S SEAFOOD BAR**
⑩ **DARN GOOD PIZZA**
⑮ **SUBWAY**

Other

③ **FOOD GIANT PLAZA**
  • Food Giant
        6am-midnight
  • Payless Drug
  • Ross
  • Midas Muffler
  • Dunkin' Donuts
  • Burger King
  • Phone
  • Cinemas

⑦ **K-MART PLAZA**
  • K-Mart
  • K-Mart Auto
  • Aurora Teriyaki
  • Jane's Cafe
  • Laundromat
  • Phone

⑨ **FIRESTONE CAR SERVICE
    CENTER**
  • 7am-6:30pm Mon-Fri,
    8am-5pm Sat, 10am-4pm
    Sun
⑬ **BROWN BEAR CAR WASH**
⑯ **NORTHGATE VETERINARY
    CLINIC**
⑰ **SAFEWAY** (24 Hrs.)

Exit 175

This exit provides access to many services. In addition to those listed, there are many more in both directions along Hwy 99.

Key Features: Food, gas

Towing:
AM-PM Towing 365-0330
Lang Towing 322-3383

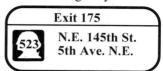

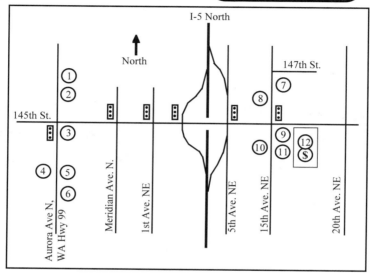

Restaurants

③ **LAS MARGARITAS** $$
11am-11pm Fri-Sat, 11am-10:30pm Sun-Thurs. Full service. Cash & credit cards. Mexican menu. Full bar.

⑦ **ITALO** $$
11am-10:30pm Mon-Thur, 11am-11pm Fri, 12pm-11pm Sat, 4pm-10:30pm Sun. Full service. Cash & credit cards. Italian menu. Full bar.

Fast Food

④ **KIDD VALLEY HAMBURGERS**
⑤ **TACO TIME**
⑥ **FISH BOWL FISH & CHIPS**
⑨ **PIZZA HUT**

⑩ **GODFATHER'S PIZZA**
⑪ **BURGER KING**

Other

① **HC AUTO CARE**
• 363-8946
② **MINIT-LUBE**
⑧ **EARL'S GARAGE**
• AAA approved
• 364-7400
• 7:30am-5:30pm, Mon-Fri
⑫ **OLSON'S PLAZA**
• Olson's Supermarket (24 Hrs.)
• Payless Drug
• Phone
• Mr. Kleen Car Wash
• Little Caesar's Pizza

Exit 176

This exit leads to a primarily residential area, although there are additional services in both directions on Hwy 99 (Aurora Avenue).

Key Features: Food, gas

Towing:
Jim's Northgate Towing 364-1500
Day & Nite Towing 633-5400

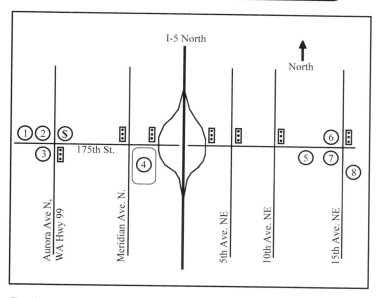

Service Stations

② **PINK PANTRY** 6am-12am
Mon-Thurs, 6am-1am Fri-Sat,
7am-12am Sun. Self-serve,
large mini-mart, cash & credit
cards, phone, espresso, ice. No
restrooms.

③ **TEXACO** 24 Hrs.
Self-serve, cash & credit cards,
restrooms, phones.

Restaurants

⑥ **PEKING HOUSE** $$
11:30am-10pm Mon-Thurs,
11:30am-11pm Fri, 12pm-11pm
Sat, 1pm-10pm Sun. 365-6500
Full service with take-out
available. Cash & credit cards.
Chinese menu. Full bar.

Other

① **FIRE DEPARTMENT**
④ **RONALD BOG PARK**
⑤ **NORTHEND AUTOMOTIVE SERVICE**
• Propane
• 361-2641
⑦ **POST OFFICE**
⑧ **SAFEWAY** (24 HRS.)

Exit 177

This exit leads to an area that is primarily residential, but there are services along Ballinger Way, 244th Street, and WA Hwy 99. You can also stop for a picnic or a little fishing at Lake Ballinger.

Key Features: Lake Ballinger, food, gas

Towing: Mary's Towing 743-5800, Ballinger Towing 363-0066

Northbound:

Exit 177
104 **Edmonds**
Mountlake Terrace

Southbound:

Exit 177
104 **N.E. 205th St.**
Lake Forest Park

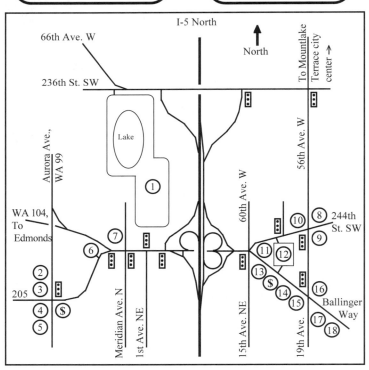

Service Stations

④ **BP** 24 Hrs.
Self-serve, small mini-mart, cash & credit cards, drive-thru car wash, restrooms with handicapped access, phone. Mechanic on duty 9am-7pm. Minor mechanical assistance from 6am-10pm.

⑦ **BP** 24 Hrs.
Self-serve, cash & credit cards, tiny mini-mart, restrooms, phones. Mechanic on duty 9:30-4:30.

⑧ **7-11 (CITGO)** 24 Hrs.
Large mini-mart, cash & credit cards, ice, cash machine.

Exit 177 *continued*

⑨ **ARCO AM/PM**   24 Hrs.
Self-serve, mini-mart, cash &
cash-machine cards, restrooms,
phone.

⑪ **TEXACO**   24 Hrs.
Self-serve, mini-mart, cash &
credit cards, diesel, restrooms
with handicapped access,
phone, ice.

⑬ **CHEVRON**   24 Hrs.
Self- & full-serve, tiny mini-
mart, cash & credit cards,
propane, restrooms, phone.
Mechanic on duty 7am-6pm
weekdays, 9am-6pm Sat.
Towing: Ballinger Towing,
363-0066.

Restaurants

⑥ **COCO'S** $$
24 Hrs. Full service & counter.
Cash & credit cards. American
menu specializing in pies. You
can purchase whole pies to take
home. Wine available.

⑰ **THE COOKHOUSE** $$
6am-10pm 7 days. 363-5051
Full service & counter with
take-out available. Cash &
credit cards. American menu.
Beer & wine available.

Fast Food

② **DENNY'S**
③ **ARBY'S**
⑤ **GODFATHER'S PIZZA**
⑮ **MCDONALD'S**

Other

① **BALLINGER PARK**
  • Picnic area
  • Fishing dock
  • Boat ramp
  • Restrooms
  • Phones

⑩ **GATEWAY AUTO REPAIR**
  • U-Haul
  • Towing: 774-1844

⑫ **BALLINGER VILLAGE**
  • Buzz Inn Steak House
  • Terrace Pharmacy
  • Food Giant
  • Sno-King Bakery
  • Subway
  • Kings III Chinese
    Restaurant
  • Kyodai Japanese
    Restaurant
  • Toshi's Teriyaki
  • Cash machine
  • Phones

⑭ **MINIT-LUBE**

⑯ **BALLINGER AUTO CLINIC**

⑱ **HUOTH-SATH PLAZA**
  • Teriyaki Plus
  • Westernco Donuts

Exit 179

This exit provides access to food, gas, and other services. There are also two parks where you can stop for a picnic or a break.

Key Features: Food, gas

Towing: Shannon Towing 774-8811, Mary's Towing 743-5800

Northbound:

Exit 179
220th St. S.W.

Southbound:

Exit 179
220th St. S.W.
Mountlake Terrace

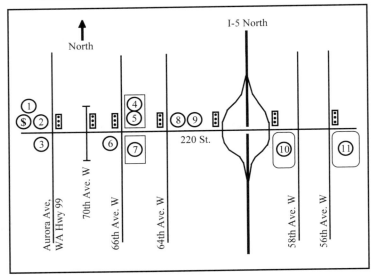

Service Stations

② **7-11 CITGO**   24 Hrs.
Self-serve, large mini-mart, cash & credit cards & checks, phone, ice, cash machine, no restrooms.

③ **TEXACO**   5am-11pm
Mon-Thurs, 5am-2am Fri, 6am-2am Sat, 6am-11pm Sun. Self-serve, cash & credit cards, mini-mart, restrooms with handicapped access, phones.

⑤ **ARCO PLAID PANTRY** 24 Hrs.
Self-serve, large mini-mart, cash & credit cards & checks, phone, no restrooms.

⑥ **TEXACO**   24 Hrs.
Self-serve, mini-mart, cash & credit cards, diesel, phone, no restrooms.

Fast Food

⑨ **7-11 HOAGY'S CORNER**

Exit 179 *continued*

Other

① **TOP FOODS** (24 HRS.)
④ **MELODY HILL VILLAGE**
  • Countryside Donut House
  • Bento Teriyaki
  • Video Adventure & Deli
  • O'Houlie's Pub
  • Thai Terrace Restaurant
  • Bloom's Cost Less
    Pharmacy
⑦ **TERRACE VILLAGE**
  • China Passage Restaurant
  • Azteca
  • Port of Subs
  • Phone
⑧ **ANIMAL CARE CENTER**
⑩ **JACK LONG PARK**
  • Picnic Area
  • (On-street parking only)
⑪ **EVERGREEN PLAYFIELD**
  • Sports fields
  • Restrooms
  • Picnic area
  • Children's play area
  • Phone

One of the many colorful vehicles you might see along the way.

Exit 181

This exit features extensive services: shopping, accommodations, food, and gas. You can reach Alderwood Mall from this exit (via Alderwood Mall Blvd.) or from Exit 182. See Exit 182 for more nearby shopping and services.

Key Features: Alderwood Mall, extensive shopping and services

Towing: Shannon Towing 774-8811, MAC Towing 776-2900

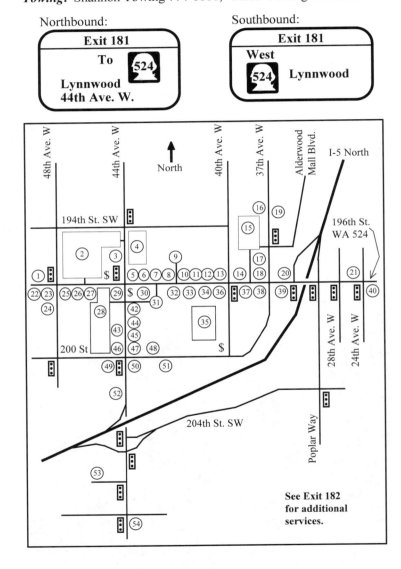

Exit 181 *continued*

Service Stations

③ **USA GASOLINE**   24 Hrs.
Self-serve, cash, phone, no restrooms.

㉑ **UNOCAL 76**   6am-9pm
Mon-Fri, 7am-9pm weekends.
Self- & full-serve, tiny mini-mart, cash & credit cards, diesel, restrooms, phone.
Mechanic on duty 9am-5pm Mon-Sat. Phone: 775-4066.

㉔ **ARCO**   5am-12am
Mon-Fri, 6am-12am Sat-Sun.
Self-serve, cash & cash-machine cards, drive-thru car wash, phone, no restrooms.

㊵ **TEXACO**   7am-11pm
Sun-Thurs, 7am-2am Fri-Sat.
Self-serve, mini-mart, cash & credit cards, ice, phone, no restrooms.

㊺ **BP CAR WASH**   24 Hrs.
Self-serve, mini-mart, cash & credit cards, diesel, do-it-yourself & drive-thru car wash, espresso, phone, no restrooms.

㊻ **TEXACO**   24 Hrs.
Self- & full-serve, tiny mini-mart, cash & credit cards, diesel, propane, restrooms with handicapped access, phone.
Mechanic on duty 8:30am-4:30pm Mon-Sat. Assistance available for tire changes, etc., 4:30pm-8pm.

㊾ **CHEVRON**   24 Hrs.
Self- & full-serve, tiny mini-mart, cash & credit cards, propane, no restrooms, phone.
AAA-approved mechanic on duty 8am-8pm weekdays, 8am-6pm weekends. Towing: R&R Star Towing (778-9557).

㊤ **ARCO AM/PM**   24 Hrs.
Self-serve, mini-mart, cash & cash-machine cards, restrooms, phones.

Restaurants

⑤ **ENG'S CHINA KITCHEN** $$
4pm-11:30pm Mon-Thurs, 4pm-2am Fri-Sat, 3pm-10pm Sun. (206) 775-1661 Full service with take-out available. Cash & credit cards & checks. Chinese menu. Full bar.

⑥ **RED LOBSTER** $$
11am-10pm Sun-Thurs, 11am-11pm Fri-Sat. Full service. Cash & credit cards. Seafood menu. Full bar.

⑦ **OLIVE GARDEN** $$
11am-10pm Sun-Thurs, 11am-11pm Fri-Sat. Full service. Cash & credit cards. Italian menu. Full bar.

⑫ **KOSTALEE'S FAMILY PASTA & PIZZA** $$
11am-10pm Sun-Thurs, 11am-11pm Fri-Sat. Full service. Cash & credit cards. Pizza, pasta, burgers, salads, gyros, chicken, & ribs.

㉕ **ASIA GARDEN** $$
11am-2am Mon-Sat, 12pm-12am Sun. (206) 775-2535 Buffet & full service, take-out available. Cash & credit cards. Chinese menu with all-you-can-eat lunch buffet. Full bar.

㉖ **APPLEBEE'S** $$
11am-1am Mon-Thurs, 11am-2am Fri-Sat, 10am-12am Sun. Full service. Cash & credit cards & checks. American menu. Full bar.

Exit 181 *continued*

③① **COUNTRY HARVEST** $$
10:45am-9pm Mon-Fri, 8am-9pm Sat, 8am-8pm Sun. Buffet. Cash & credit cards. American menu.

③⑥ **THE YANKEE DINER** $$
7am-10pm Mon-Sat, 8am-9pm Sun. Full service. Cash & credit cards. American menu featuring pot roast, home-made pies, soups, preserves. Full bar.

③⑦ **TONY ROMA'S** $$
11am-10pm Sun-Thurs, 11am-11pm Fri-Sat. Full service. Cash & credit cards & checks. BBQ menu. Full bar.

③⑨ **TAKI** $$
11:30am-2am Mon-Fri, 5pm-9pm Sat, closed Sun. Full service with take-out available. Cash & credit cards. Authentic, reasonably priced Japanese menu. Beer & wine available. Be sure to try their ginger or green tea ice cream!

④③ **EL TORITO** $$
11am-10pm Mon-Thurs, 11am-11pm Fri-Sat, 10am-9pm Sun. Full service. Cash & credit cards. Mexican menu. Full bar.

④④ **GREAT CHINA** $$
11am-9:30pm Mon-Thurs, 11am-10:30pm Fri, 2pm-10:30pm Sat, 2pm-9:30pm Sun. Full service with take-out available. Cash & credit cards. Chinese menu.

④⑦ **COCO'S** $$
6am-11pm Sun-Thurs, 6am-12am Fri-Sat. Full and counter service. Cash & credit cards. American menu specializing in pies. You can buy whole pies to take out. Beer & wine available.

④⑧ **NEON MOON** $$
11am-10pm Mon-Fri, 4:30pm-10pm Sat-Sun. Full service. Cash & credit cards. American menu. Full bar. Live country dancing.

⑤② **BLACK ANGUS** $$
11am-10pm Mon-Thurs, 11am-11pm Fri-Sat, 12pm-10pm Sun. Full service. Cash & credit cards. American menu featuring steak. Full bar.

Fast Food

① **PIZZA HUT**
⑩ **DENNY'S**
⑪ **BASKIN-ROBBINS**
⑬ **KENTUCKY FRIED CHICKEN**
⑲ **McDONALD'S**
㉒ **ARBY'S**
㉓ **ALFY'S PIZZA**
㉘ **JACK IN THE BOX**
㉚ **SUBWAY**
㉜ **INTERNATIONAL HOUSE OF PANCAKES**
㉝ **BURGER KING**
㊳ **TACO TIME**

Lodging

⑨ **HOLIDAY INN EXPRESS**
(206) 775-8030 ☺☺☺ $$$
Cash & credit cards. Discounts available. Kids under 19 free in room with parents. Non-smoking & handicapped rooms available. Phone, cable TV. Some rooms have refrigerators. Indoor spa. Coffee, snack machines, & microwave in "great room" area in lobby. Continental breakfast. Guest laundry. No pets.

Exit 181 *continued*

⑯ **Silver Cloud Inn** ☺☺ $$$
(206) 775-7600 Cash & credit cards. Discounts available. Pets OK with fee. Non-smoking & handicapped rooms available. Phone, cable TV, refrigerators. Outdoor heated pool, indoor & outdoor spa. Continental breakfast & coffee in lobby. Guest laundry. Conference rooms. Fax available. Very nice lobby. Truck parking available.

㊿ **Best Western Landmark Inn** 1-800-528-1234 ☺☺☺ $$$
Cash & credit cards & checks. Discounts available. Non-smoking & handicapped rooms available. Elevators. Phones, cable TV. Indoor pool & spa. Laundry service. Meeting rooms & ballroom. *Attached restaurant:* The Mark $$.

(53) **Embassy Suites** ☺☺☺ $$$$
(206) 775-2500 Cash & credit cards & checks. Discounts available. Non-smoking & handicapped rooms available. All suites. No pets. Phone, cable TV with Showtime & pay-per-view movies, kitchenettes, guest laundry, concierge, gift shop, meeting rooms, shuttle within a 5-mile radius. Full breakfast (cooked to order) & complimentary drinks included. Large central atrium with garden & running stream. Heated indoor pool with exercise area, spa, sauna.
Attached restaurant:
McCarthy's Restaurant & Lounge $$$ Seafood, full bar.

Other

② **Fred Meyer**
- Tire Center

④ **Highline Plaza**
- Tsuruya Japanese Restaurant
- Happy Teriyaki
- Highline Cleaners
- Dave's Burgers
- Highline Food Store
- Phone

⑧ **Bosley's Pet Food**

⑭ **Alderwood Veterinary Clinic**

⑮ **Alderwood Village**
- Drug Emporium
- Chuck E Cheese
- Hancock Fabrics
- Chinese Delight Restaurant
- Cinemas
- Macheezmo Mouse Mexican Restaurant

⑰ **Econo Lube n Tune**

⑱ **Matrix Mufflers & Brakes**

⑳ **Kinko's**
- 24-hour copies & fax

㉗ **Firestone Tire Center**
- 7am-7pm Mon-Fri, 8am-5pm Sat, 10am-4pm Sun

㉘ **Lynnwood Square**
- Fabricland
- Jack in the Box
- Hawaii BBQ
- Wherehouse
- Car Toys
- Skipper's
- Cash machine
- Phone

㉞ **Super Shops Car Care**

㉟ **Wood World Mall**
- Wood World Furniture
- Sandwich Aisle
- Jones & Co. Pets
- Phones

㊶ **Car-Tec Auto Repair**
- 774-1450

㊷ **Good Year Auto Service**
- 7:30am-6pm Mon-Fri, 8am-5pm Sat, 10am-4pm Sun

(51) **Centers 3 Collision Center** (car repair)

Exit 182

Northbound, this exit leads to the shopping area around the Alderwood Mall (which has just about every store imaginable) or to I-405 South to Bellevue and other towns on the East side of Lake Washington. *Southbound exits to I-405 only.* Southbound take Exit 181 to reach Alderwood Mall. See Exit 181 for additional services.

Key Features: SHOPPING!!!

Towing: Shannon Towing 774-8811, MAC Towing 776-2900

Northbound:

Exit 182	
525 North To **99**	**INTERSTATE 405** South **Bellevue Renton**

Southbound:

Exit 182
INTERSTATE 405 South **Bellevue Renton**

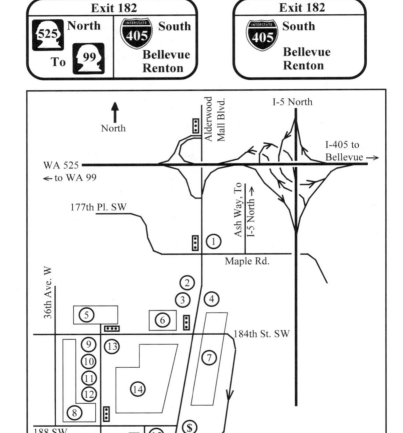

Exit 182 *continued*

Service Stations

① **ARCO AM/PM**   24 Hrs.
Self-serve, mini-mart, cash &
cash-machine cards, restroom,
phone.

Restaurants

② **THE KEG** $$
11am-10pm Mon-Thurs, 11am-
11pm Fri-Sat, 11am-9:30pm
Sun. Full service. Cash & credit
cards. American menu featuring
steak & seafood. Full bar.

⑨ **RED ROBIN** $$
11am-11pm Mon-Thur, 11am-
1:30am Fri-Sat, 11am-10:30pm
Sun. Full service. Cash & credit
cards. Great burgers. Full bar.

⑩ **BILLY MCHALE'S** $$
11am-9:30pm Mon, 11am-10pm
Tues-Thurs, 11am-11pm Fri-
Sat, 11am-9pm Sun. Full
service. Cash & credit cards.
American menu. Full bar.

Fast Food

⑪ **GODFATHER'S PIZZA**
⑫ **SKIPPER'S**

Lodging

③ **RESIDENCE INN** ☺☺☺ $$$
1-800-331-3131 or 771-1100
Cash & credit cards. Discounts,
weekly/monthly rates available.
Non-smoking & handicapped
rooms available. All suites,
featuring full kitchens with
dining counter, living room
with fireplace (firewood
available), phone, cable TV.
Continental breakfast, evening
snacks, coffee in room. Picnic
& BBQ area. Grocery shopping
service available. Guest

laundry. Conference rooms.
Video rentals. Safe deposit
boxes available. Van to local
restaurants & shopping. Pets
OK with fee. Outdoor heated
pool, exercise area, spas, sport
court.

Other

④ **ALDERWOOD AUTO SERVICE
   CENTER**

⑤ **MERVYN'S PLAZA**
   • Mervyn's
   • California Burgers
   • Alderwood Cinemas
   • Elmer's Pancake & Steak
     House
   • Cash machine
   • Phone

⑥ **PACIFIC LINEN PLAZA**
   • Pacific Linen
   • Picway Shoes
   • Lenscrafters
   • Men's Wearhouse
   • TCBY Yogurt
   • Dahle's Big & Tall

⑦ **TARGET PLAZA**
   • Target
   • Toys-R-Us
   • NW Mail (fax, copies)
   • Katie's Deli & Teriyaki
   • Grand Cinemas
   • Boehm's Chocolate
   • Western Optical
   • Cost-Plus Imports
   • Extra Space
   • Exercise Equipment Ctr.

⑧ **ALDERWOOD PLAZA**
   • Office Max
   • Dolphin Pet
   • QFC (24 Hrs.)
   • Nippon Restaurant
   • Payless Drug
   • PioPio's Restaurant
   • Big 5 Sporting Goods
   • Several other shops

Exit 182 *continued*

⑬ **ALDERWOOD CORNER**
- Pacific Vision
- Vets for Less Animal
  Clinic
- Sizzler

⑭ **ALDERWOOD MALL**
- JC Penney
- Lamont's
- Nordstrom
- Sears (with Auto Center)
- KB Toys
- The Bon
- Many, many other stores
  & eating places

⑮ **SILO PLAZA**
- Silo
- See's Candies
- Waterbed Emporium

⑯ **ALDERWOOD HOME
   FURNISHING CENTER**
- Azteca
- Healthy Way Nutrition
  Center
- Ross
- The Bon Home Store
- Scan Design
- The Bedroom Store

⑰ **ALDERWOOD TOWNE
   CENTER**
- Pier 1 Imports
- Pastry Cafe
- Pella Window Store
- Nordstrom Rack
- Marshall's
- Abodio
- Calico Corners Fabrics
- National Luggage Outlet
- Shoe Pavilion
- Nu Yu Wholesale
  Fashions
- Clothestime
- Smart Size
- Modern Woman

Exit 183

This exit is primarily residential. However, you can reach Alderwood Mall from this exit and food and gas are available.

Key Features: Food, gas, access to Alderwood Mall

Towing:
South Co. Towing 743-4810
R&R Star Towing 778-9557

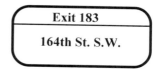

Exit 183

164th St. S.W.

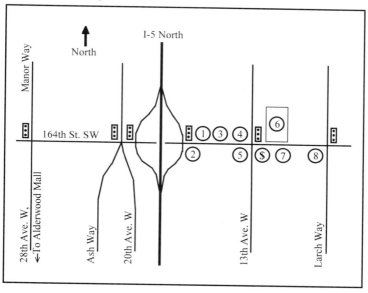

Service Stations

② **CHEVRON**   24 Hrs.
Self-serve, mini-mart, cash & credit cards & checks.

③ **ARCO AM/PM**   24 Hrs.
Self-serve, cash & cash-machine cards, restrooms, phones.

④ **TEXACO**   24 Hrs.
Self-serve, large mini-mart, cash & credit cards, diesel, drive-thru car wash, ice, restrooms with handicapped access, phone.

⑤ **UNOCAL 76**   6am-10pm
7 days. Self- & full-serve, cash & credit cards, propane, phone. Mechanic on duty 8am-4pm 7 days.

Fast Food

⑦ **JACK IN THE BOX**
⑧ **TACO TIME**

Other

① **CAR-TEC**
  • 8am-6pm Mon-Fri, 8am-5pm Sat, closed Sun

⑥ **MARTHA LAKE PLAZA**
  • Subway
  • Ashiya Restaurant
  • 13th Ave Pub & Eatery
  • Jacques Deli
  • Phone

Exit 186

This exit provides plenty of places to eat & stay overnight. You can also relax for awhile in McCollum Park, if you're just ready for a break.

Key Features: Food, services, and McCollum Park

Towing:
Inter-County Towing 745-2266
Ron May Towing 259-9264

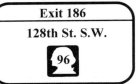

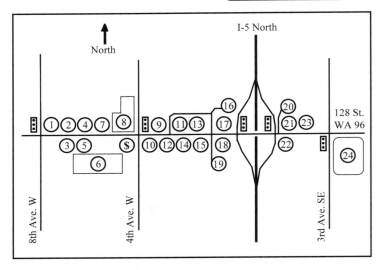

Service Stations

① ARCO AM/PM   24 Hrs.
Self-serve, mini-mart, cash & cash-machine cards, phone.

⑧ 7-11   24 Hrs.
Self-serve, cash & credit cards & checks, large mini-mart, phones, espresso, cash machine.

⑬ TEXACO   24 Hrs.
Self-serve, mini-mart, cash & credit cards, drive-thru car wash, espresso, restrooms, phone.

⑮ CHEVRON   24 Hrs.
Self-serve, mini-mart, cash & credit cards, phone, restrooms with handicapped access.

㉑ TEXACO   24 Hrs.
Self-serve, tiny mini-mart, cash & credit cards, diesel, restrooms with handicapped access, ice, phone.

㉒ BP   24 Hrs.
Self-serve, mini-mart, propane, cash & credit cards, restrooms, phone, mechanic available 9am-6pm Mon-Fri, 8am-5pm Sat.

Restaurants

③ GREAT RIVER $$
3pm-12am Mon, 11am-12am Tues-Thurs, 11am-2am Fri, 3pm-2am Sat, 3pm-10:30pm Sun. Full service with take-out available. Cash & credit cards. Chinese menu. Full bar.

Exit 186 *continued*

⑨ **MITZEL'S** $$
6am-11pm Sun-Thur, 6am-
12pm Fri-Sat. Full service.
Cash & credit cards & checks.
American menu, featuring pies
& fresh turkey. Beer & wine
available.

Fast Food

④ TACO BELL
⑤ McDONALD'S
⑦ PIZZA HUT
⑩ SKIPPER'S
⑪ KENTUCKY FRIED CHICKEN
⑭ DAIRY QUEEN
⑰ BURGER KING
⑱ DENNY'S

Lodging

⑯ **CYPRESS INN** ☺☺ $$$
(206)347-9099 or 1-800-752-
9991 #3. Non-smoking &
handicapped rooms available.
Elevators. Cash & credit cards
& checks. Discounts available.
Phones, cable TV, all rooms
have refrigerators. Pets OK
with fee. Outdoor heated pool.
Video rentals, microwave
available in lobby. Safe deposit
boxes available. Meeting rooms
and fax available. Continental
breakfast in lobby.

⑲ **MOTEL 6** ☺ $$
(206) 353-8120 Non-smoking
& handicapped rooms available.
Cash & credit cards. Cable TV
with HBO, phones. Pets OK.
Friendly, quiet.

㉓ **HOLIDAY INN** ☺☺☺ $$$
(206) 745-2555 Non-smoking
& handicapped rooms available.
Elevators. Cash & credit cards
& checks. Discounts available.
Phones, cable TV, some
refrigerators available. Pets OK
with fee. Some family suites
available. Laundry service. Van
available for local transportation.
Indoor heated pool & spa with
exercise area. Safe deposit
boxes available. Meeting rooms
available. *Attached restaurant:*
Terrace Cafe. Bar overlooks
pool area.

Other

② GOODYEAR AUTO CENTER
  • 745-4134 or 348-4270
⑥ PUGET PARK MALL
  • Yummy Teriyaki
  • Taco Time
  • 99-cent Store
  • Radio Shack
  • Albertson's (24 Hrs.)
  • Phone
  • Craft Outlet
⑧ **7-11 MALL**
  • 7-11 (See details under
      Service Stations)
  • Alfy's Pizza
  • Big Wheel Auto Parts
  • Teriyaki Plus
  • My Kitchen Bakery
  • Cash machine
⑫ MINIT LUBE
⑳ VISITOR INFORMATION
   CENTER (in gas station
   parking lot)
㉔ McCOLLUM PARK
  • Public outdoor pool
  • Volleyball
  • Covered picnic area
  • Restrooms
  • Sports fields
  • Children's play area
  • Stream, woods
  • Walking trails
  • Phone

Exit 189

This exit provides access to Everett, Mukilteo, Whidbey Island Ferry, and the Everett Mall, with plenty of shopping and other services.

Key Features: Everett Mall, Whidbey Island Ferry
Towing: Ron May Towing 269-9264, Skip's Towing 259-2981

Northbound:

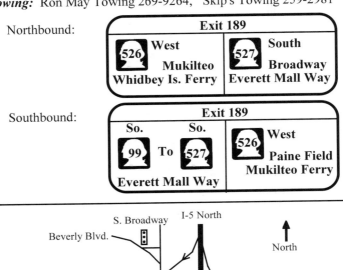

Southbound:

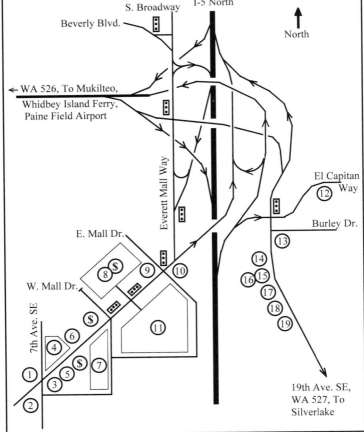

Exit 189 *continued*

Service Stations

① **COUNTRY PUMP / BP** 4:30am-12am Mon-Wed, 4:30am-2am Thurs-Sat, 6am-12am Sun. Self-serve, large mini-mart, cash & credit cards & checks, phone.

② **TEXACO** 24 Hrs. Self-serve, large mini-mart, cash & credit cards, phones.

⑫ **TEXACO** 6:30am-9pm Mon-Fri, 8am-8pm Sat, closed Sun. Self-serve, mini-mart, cash & credit cards, phone. Mechanic on duty 9am-6pm Mon-Fri.

⑬ **TEXACO** 24 Hrs. Self- & full-serve, mini-mart, cash & credit cards, phone, propane, drive-thru car wash, restrooms with handicapped access. Mechanic on duty 7:30am-5:30pm Tues-Sat.

⑮ **ARCO** 5am-12am Mon-Fri, 7am-2am Sat-Sun. Self-serve, mini-mart, cash, ice, phone.

Restaurants

⑭ **BUZZ INN STEAK HOUSE** $$ 6am-2am Mon-Sat, 7am-12am Sun. Full service. Cash & credit cards. Burgers, steak.

⑯ **ORCHID** $$ 11am-9:30pm Mon-Thurs, 11am-10pm Fri, 4pm-10pm Sat, 4pm-9:30pm Sun. Full service. Cash & credit cards. Thai menu. Full bar.

Fast Food

⑤ **DAIRY QUEEN**
⑥ **RAX**
⑨ **JACK IN THE BOX**
⑱ **ALFY'S PIZZA**

Lodging

⑩ **COMFORT INN** ☺☺ $$ (206) 355-1570 Non-smoking rooms available. Cash & credit cards & checks. Discounts available. Cable TV, refrigerators, phone, coffee in rooms. No pets. Two family suites available. Cleaning service & laundry available. Outdoor heated pool & spa. Continental breakfast.

⑰ **RAMADA INN** ☺☺☺ $$$ (206) 337-9090 Non-smoking & handicapped rooms available. Cash & credit cards. Discounts & weekly rates available. Phones, cable TV with HBO. Some refrigerators available. Heated outdoor pool & spa. Pets OK. Continental breakfast. Video rentals available. Fax, meeting rooms. Friendly staff.

Other

③ **MIDAS MUFFLER**

④ **909 BUSINESS CENTER**
  • Godfather's Pizza
  • EBM (fax, copiers, etc.)
  • AAA Washington

⑦ **EVERETT MALL VILLAGE**
  • Cash machine
  • North Gardens Chinese Restaurant
  • Discovery Zone (play place for kids)
  • Laundromat
  • Cinemas
  • Phone

Exit 189 *continued*

⑧ **EVERETT MALL PLAZA**
- Top Foods (24 Hrs.)
- Toys-R-Us
- Sparks Tune-Up
  (7am-7pm Mon-Fri)
- Petco
- Big 5 Sporting Goods
- Starbucks Coffee
- Red Robin
- Azteca
- Olive Garden
- Pier 1 Imports

⑪ **EVERETT MALL**
- The Bon (with Tire Center)
- Payless Drug
- Food Court
- Sears (with Auto Center)
- Cinemas
- Mervyn's
- Many other shops

⑲ **ROLLERFAIR SKATE DECK**
(rollerskating)

I-5 looking South from Exit 168A with
the Space Needle in the background.

Truck Weigh Station

Northbound: At mile-marker 188, the truck weigh station provides a safe place to stop and phones.

Weigh Station and Rest Area

Southbound: At mile-marker 188, is a truck weigh station and the Silver Creek Rest Area, featuring:

- RV pumpout
- Free Coffee
- Potable water
- Phones
- Handicapped restrooms
- Picnic area
- Tourist Information

Exit 192

This exit leads to Everett city center and the next several exits northbound via Broadway.

Key Features: Everett city center.

Towing: Ron May Towing 259-9264,   Dick's Towing 252-4004

Northbound *left-hand* exit:

Exit 192
Broadway **City Center**

Southbound:

Exit 192
41st St. **Evergreen Way**

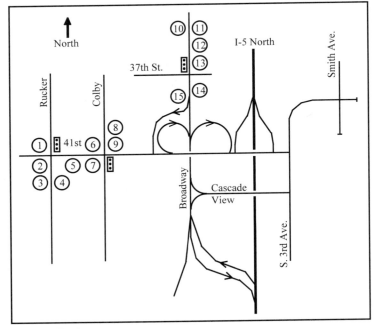

Service Stations

① **ARCO**   24 Hrs. Self-serve, mini-mart, cash & cash-machine cards, phone.

② **BP**   5am-12am 7days. Self-serve, mini-mart, cash & credit cards. Mechanic available 8am-5pm Mon-Sat.

⑨ **TEXACO**   5am-12am Mon-Fri, 7am-12am Sat-Sun. Self-serve, large mini-mart, cash & credit cards, espresso, propane, ice, phones.

⑩ **ARCO /JACKPOT FOOD MART**   24 Hrs. Self-serve, large mini-mart, cash, espresso, phone.

⑪ **BP**   8am-8pm Mon-Sat, 9am-7pm Sun. Self-serve, cash & credit cards, phone, drive-thru & do-it-yourself car wash.

Exit 192 *continued*

Restaurants

⑤ **41ST ST. BAR & GRILL** $$
6am-9pm Sun-Thurs, 8am-10pm
Fri-Sat. (206) 259-3838 Full
service. Cash & credit cards.
Burgers & steak. Full bar.

⑬ **BUZZ INN STEAKHOUSE** $$
6am-1am Mon-Sat, 7am-12am
Sun. Full service. Cash & credit
cards. Steak. Full bar.

Fast Food

④ **KENTUCKY FRIED CHICKEN**
⑥ **MCDONALD'S**
⑦ **IVAR'S SEAFOOD BAR**
⑧ **BASKIN-ROBBINS**
⑮ **KING'S TABLE**

Other

③ **SAFEWAY**
  • 6am-12am 7 days
  • Phone

⑫ **MINIT-LUBE**

⑭ **PACIFIC POWER BATTERIES**
  • Propane
  • U-Haul rentals
  • Phone

Exit 193

This is a *Northbound* exit only, leading to Everett city center by way of Pacific Ave. See Exit 194, via Broadway, for additional services and a Northbound entrance.

Key Features: Everett city center, food, gas, & lodging

Towing:
Skip's Towing 259-2981
Mid-City Towing 339-2663

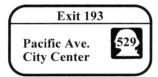

Exit 193	
Pacific Ave. **City Center**	529

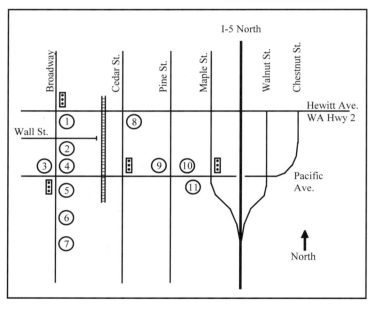

Service Stations

④ **BP** 24 Hrs.
Self-serve, mini-mart, cash & credit cards, restrooms, phone.

⑤ **CHEVRON** 24 Hrs.
Self- & full-serve, cash & credit cards, propane, phones, restrooms. Mechanic available 7am-5pm, 7 days.

⑧ **BP** 5:30am-10pm Mon-Fri, 7am-10pm Sat, 7am-9pm Sun. Self-serve, large mini-mart with deli & hot food, cash & credit cards, diesel, espresso, ice, phone.

Restaurants

② **CHINA DOLL** $$
11am-1:45am Mon-Thurs, 11am-2:45am Fri-Sat, Noon-10:45pm Sun. Full service with take-out available. Cash & credit cards. Chinese menu. Full bar.

⑥ **PETOSA'S** $$
7am-11pm Mon-Thur, 7am-12am Fri-Sat, 7am-10pm Sun. Full service & counter. Cash & credit cards. American menu. Full bar.

⑦ **NEW PEKING** $$
11:30am-10pm Mon-Thurs,
11:30am-11pm Fri, Noon-11pm
Sat, 4pm-10pm Sun. Full
service with take-out available.
Cash & credit cards. Chinese
menu.

Fast Food

⑩ **DENNY'S**

Lodging

③ **TRAVELODGE**   ☺☺ $$$
(206) 259-6141 Non-smoking
rooms available. Cash & credit
cards. Discounts available. Cable
TV with Showtime, phones,
coffee in room. No pets.

⑨ **NENDEL'S INN** ☺☺☺ $$$
1-800-547-0106 Local: (206)
258-4141 Cash & credit cards
& checks. Discounts available.
Non-smoking & handicapped
rooms available. Elevators.
Phones, cable TV with
Showtime, refrigerators, coffee
in room. Free local phone calls.
Family suites available.
Outdoor heated pool & spa.
Exercise area. Pets OK with
fee. Guest laundry & dry
cleaning pickup available. Safe
deposit boxes available.
Continental breakfast in lobby.
Fax machine. Banquet facilities.
Friendly, helpful staff. *Attached
restaurant:*   Kate's Spirits &
Eatery $$ 11am-9pm Mon-
Thurs, 11am-10:30pm Fri, 5pm-
10:30pm Sat, 4pm-8pm Sun.
Sun brunch: 10am-2pm. Full
bar.

⑪ **EVERETT PACIFIC HOTEL**
(206) 339-3333   ☺☺☺ $$$
or 1-800-426-0670 Cash &
credit cards & checks. Discounts
available. Non-smoking &
handicapped rooms available.
Phones, refrigerators. Family
suites available. Indoor heated
pool, spa, & exercise area. No
pets. Guest laundry & dry
cleaning service available.
Meeting rooms available.
Shuttle to shopping. *Attached
restaurant:* Hardy's $$$ Full
bar, live entertainment Tues-Sat.

Other

① **MORGAN-JOHNSON TRUCK
   & RV SERVICE CENTER**
   • 259-5470
   • 8am-5pm Mon-Fri

Exit 194

Northbound, this is an exit to Route 2 East to Wenatchee *only*. Southbound, you can exit either to Route 2 or Everett. There are many shops and services available along Broadway, which connects all the Everett exits.

Key Features: Rte. 2 East and Everett center

Towing: Inter-County Towing 745-2266, Skip's Towing 259-2981

Northbound: Southbound:

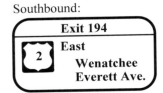

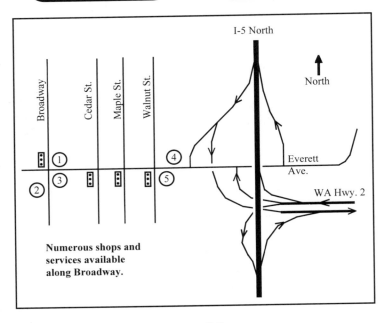

Service Stations

④ **TEXACO** 24 Hrs.
Self-serve, mini-mart, cash & credit cards, diesel, drive-thru car wash, restrooms with handicapped access, ice, phone.

Fast Food

② **KENTUCKY FRIED CHICKEN**
③ **JACK IN THE BOX**

Other

① **OLSON'S FOODS** (24 Hrs.)
⑤ **LES SCHWAB TIRES**

Exit 195

This is a *Northbound* exit only, leading to a largely residential area and a park. There are services along Broadway, approximately 1 1/2 miles from the exit. There are no services close to the exit.

Key Features: Senator Henry M. Jackson Park, phone

Towing:
Skip's Towing 259-2981
Inter-County Towing 745-2266

Exit 195

**Port of Everett
Marine View Dr.**

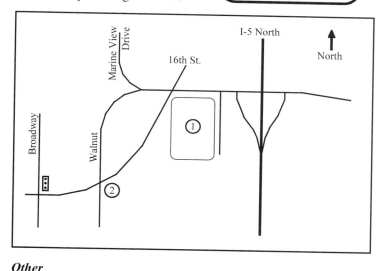

Other

① **SENATOR HENRY M. JACKSON PARK**
  • Sports fields
  • Children's play area

② **PHONE**

Exit 198

This is a *Southbound* exit only, leading to Everett via WA 529 South. There are no services near the exit. WA 529 becomes Broadway once you're in Everett. See the Everett exits for additional information.

Key Features: No services

Towing:
Skip's Towing 259-2981
Inter-County Towing 745-2266

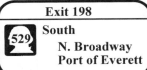

Exit 198
529 **South**
N. Broadway
Port of Everett

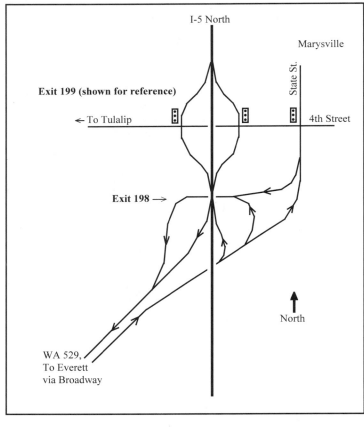

Lynch's Trading Post, Exit 199

Exit 199

This exit leads east to Marysville or west to the Tulalip Casino. There are numerous shops & services northbound on State Street.

Key Features: Marysville, Tulalip Casino, services

Towing:
Soper Towing 659-8771
Dick's Towing 653-5845

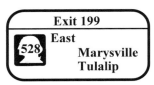

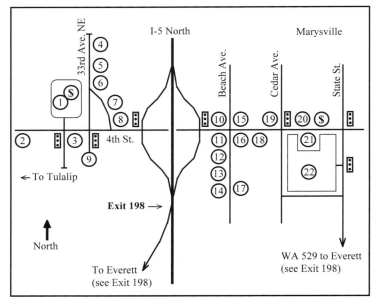

Service Stations

(8) **UNOCAL 76**   24 Hrs.
Self- & full-serve, cash & credit cards, propane, RV pump-out, espresso, restrooms, phone. Mechanic on duty 8am-5pm Mon-Fri, 8am-4pm Sat.

(11) **ARCO AM/PM**   24 Hrs.
Self-serve, cash & cash-machine cards, restrooms, phones.

(15) **TEXACO**   24 Hrs.
Self-serve, mini-mart, cash & credit cards, diesel, propane, restrooms with handicapped access, phone. Mechanic on duty 8am-5pm Mon-Fri. Jim's Texaco Towing: 659-6626.

(16) **CHEVRON**   24 Hrs.
Self-serve, mini-mart, cash & credit cards, phone.

(19) **BP**   5am-11pm 7 days.
Self-serve, tiny mini-mart, cash & credit cards, drive-thru car wash, restrooms, phone. Mechanic on duty 8am-8pm 7 days.

Restaurants

(12) **LAS MARGARITAS** $$
11am-10:30pm Sun-Thurs, 11am-11pm Fri-Sat. Full service. Cash & credit cards. Mexican menu. Full bar.

Exit 199 *continued*

⑬ **VILLAGE** $$
24 Hrs. Full service. Cash & credit cards. American menu featuring steak & seafood & pies. Full bar.

⑰ **GA MAXWELL'S** $$
7am-11pm 7 days. Full & counter service. Cash & credit cards. American menu featuring steak, pasta, & dessert. Full bar with many exotic beers on tap.

⑱ **DON'S** $$
6am-10pm 7 days. Full & counter service. Cash & credit cards. American menu. Full bar.

Fast Food

③ **ARBY'S**
⑤ **WENDY'S**
⑥ **TACO TIME**
⑦ **MCDONALD'S**
⑩ **JACK IN THE BOX**
⑳ **BURGER KING**
㉑ **DAIRY QUEEN**

Lodging

⑨ **TULALIP INN** ☺☺☺ $$$
(206) 659-4488 Cash & credit cards & checks. Discounts & weekly rates available. Non-smoking & handicapped rooms & family suites available. Phone, cable TV with HBO. Some rooms have refrigerators & microwaves. Indoor heated pool & spa. Coffee in lobby. Dry cleaning service during the week. Bellingham-SeaTac

Airporter service. Video rentals. Meeting rooms available. Canadian currency exchange. Pets OK with fee. Live jazz on Sunday nights. Friendly, helpful staff. *Attached restaurant:* Henry's Lady Restaurant & Lounge: $$$.

⑭ **VILLAGE MOTOR INN**
(206) 659-0005 ☺☺☺ $$$
Cash & credit cards & checks. Discounts available. Non-smoking & handicapped rooms & suites with spas available. Elevators. Phones, cable TV, continental breakfast, coffee in lobby. Microwave & refrigerator available. Laundry pickup during the week. Canadian currency exchange. *Attached restaurant:* Village Restaurant (reviewed separately).

Other

① **TULALIP CASINO**
• Las Vegas-style casino
• Bingo
• Cash machine
• Restaurant: 11am-11pm Sun-Thurs, 11am-12am Fri-Sat. Full service, American menu. Full bar. ($$)

② **LYNCH'S TRADING PORT**
• Indian art, jewelry, antiques

④ **ROY ROBINSON RV SALES & SERVICE**

㉒ **MARYSVILLE MALL**
• Albertson's (24 Hrs.)
• Payless
• Phone
• Lamont's
• Cafe Court
• Royal Fork Buffet
• Many other stores

Visitor Information Center

Southbound: There is a Washington State Visitor Information Center with information on things to do or see, along with pay phones, at mile-marker 201.

_____   _____
_____   _____
_____   _____
_____   _____
_____   _____
_____   _____
_____   _____
_____   _____
_____   _____
_____   _____
_____   _____
_____   _____

Wintertime on the Highway (vicinity of Everett).

Exit 202

This exit leads to a residential area with only a few services. See adjoining exits for additional services.

Key Features: Gas

Towing:
Plaza Towing 435-2361
Dick's Towing 653-5845

Exit 202

116th St. N.E.

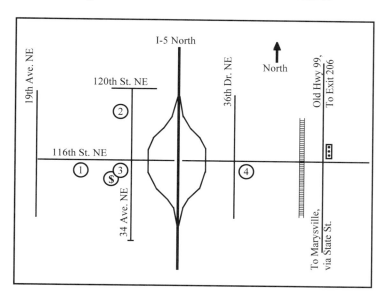

Service Stations

③ **DONNA'S BP**　　24 Hrs.
Self-serve, mini-mart with hot food & seating area, cash & credit cards, diesel, CAT-certified truck scales, truck fueling area, picnic table, ice, espresso, plenty of truck parking, UPS & Federal Express drop-offs, phone. No restrooms.

④ **CHEVRON**　　24 Hrs.
Self-serve, large mini-mart (116th St. Deli), cash & credit cards, diesel, restrooms, phones.

Other

① **WASHINGTON STATE PATROL**
• Phone

② **SUBURBAN PROPANE**
• 8am-5pm Mon-Fri,
  8am-Noon Sat
• 659-1251

Exit 206

This exit provides access to Arlington Airport, as well as numerous services.

Key Features: Arlington Airport, food, gas, & lodging.

Towing:
Plaza Towing 435-2361
Dick's Towing 653-5845

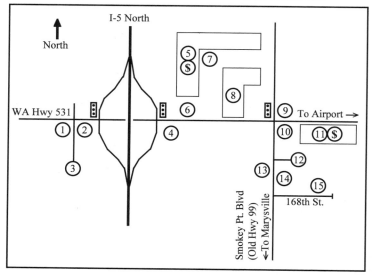

Service Stations

① SMOKEY POINT MINI MART
24 Hrs. Self-serve, large mini-mart, cash & credit cards, phone.

④ TEXACO   24 Hrs.
Self-serve, mini-mart, cash & credit cards, restrooms, phone.

⑨ ARCO AM/PM   24 Hrs.
Self-serve, mini-mart, cash & cash machine cards, restrooms, phone.

⑩ 7-11/CITGO   24 Hrs.
Self-serve, mini-mart, cash & credit cards & checks, phone, ice, cash machine.

⑭ UNOCAL 76 / MR. KLEEN CAR WASH / PAUL'S AUTO SUPPLY / 10-MIN. LUBE
6am-10pm Mon-Fri, 8am-10pm Sat, 9am-9pm Sun. Paul's Auto Supply open 8am-5:30pm Mon-Fri, 8:30am-5pm Sat, closed Sun. Self-serve, small mini-mart, cash & credit cards, diesel, propane, RV pump-out, do-it-yourself car wash, restrooms, phone.

Restaurants

② PETOSA'S $$
6am-11pm 7 days. Full- and counter service. Cash & credit cards. American & Italian menu, specializing in steak & seafood. Full bar.

⑥ **BUZZ-IN STEAKHOUSE** $$
6am-12am Mon-Sat, 6am-11pm
Sun. Full- and counter service.
Cash & credit cards. American
menu specializing in steak. Full
bar.

⑮ **PARAISO** $$
9am-9pm Mon-Fri, 9am-10pm
Sat, 9am-8pm Sun. Full-service
restaurant. Mexican menu. Cash
& credit cards.

Fast Food

⑧ **TACO TIME**
⑪ **JACK IN THE BOX**
⑫ **BOSLEY'S BBQ**

Lodging

⑦ **SMOKEY POINT MOTOR INN**
Reviewers not permitted to see
rooms. (206) 659-8561 Cash &
credit cards. Phones, cable TV,
outdoor seasonal pool.

Other

③ **SMOKEY POINT RV PARK**
   (Park Washington)
   • Office hours: 9am-5pm
   • Phones
   • Hookups
   • Children's playground
   • Recreation hall
   • Showers

⑤ **SMOKEY POINT MALL**
   • Cash Machine
   • Olympia Pizza House
   • Phone
   • Las Coronas Mexican
      Restaurant
   • Wayne's Family
      Restaurant
   • Post Office
   • Max Foods

⑧ **SMOKEY POINT PLAZA**
   • Taco Time
   • Home Plate Deli
   • Take 'n Bake Pizza

⑪ **GATEWAY CENTER**
   • Safeway (24 hrs)
   • Phones
   • Payless Drug Store
   • Pet store
   • True Value Hardware
   • Cash Machine
   • Jack in the Box

⑬ **SMOKEY POINT ANIMAL
   HOSPITAL**

Scenery is spectacular at many rest areas. Here, you see the stump of an enormous old tree - large enough to walk through or even camp in!

Truck Weigh Station

Northbound: At mile-marker 188, the truck weigh station
                  provides a safe place to stop and phones. No
                  other services.

Smokey Point Rest Area

Southbound: The Smokey Point Rest Area at mile-marker 208
                  provides the following services:

                  • RV pumpout
                  • Free Coffee
                  • Potable water
                  • Restrooms
                  • Phones

Northbound: At mile-marker 207, The Smokey Point Rest
                  Area provides:

                  • RV pumpout
                  • Free Coffee
                  • Potable water
                  • Restrooms
                  • Travel Information
                  • Vending Machines
                  • Phones

Exit 208

This exit leads to Arlington, Silvana, or the North Cascades Hwy via WA 530.

Key Features: Food, gas, lodging

Towing: Plaza Towing 652-8488, Brandt's Towing 653-6454

Northbound:

Southbound:

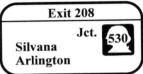

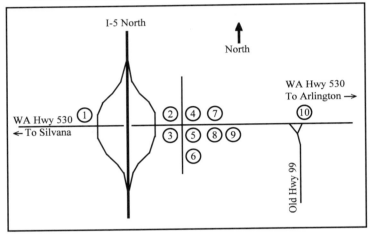

Service Stations

① **ARLINGTON FUEL STOP** 24 Hrs. Self-serve, cash & credit cards, diesel, restrooms, phone, propane.

④ **CHEVRON** 24 Hrs. Self-serve, mini-mart, cash & credit cards, restrooms with handicapped access, propane, phone, picnic tables.

⑤ **ARCO AM/PM** Under construction.

⑦ **BP** 24 Hrs. Self-serve, mini-mart, cash & credit cards & checks, phone, restrooms, espresso. Towing by Kazen's Towing 652-8700.

⑨ **TEXACO** 24 Hrs. Self-serve, mini-mart, cash & credit cards, diesel, restrooms, phone.

Restaurants

② **WELLER'S CHALET** $$ 6am-12am Mon-Thurs, 6am-1am Fri-Sat, 6am-10:30pm Sun. Full & counter service. Take-out available. Cash & credit cards. American menu. Full bar.

⑧ **O'BRIEN TURKEY HOUSE** $$ 7am-8pm. Full service, entirely non-smoking restaurant. Cash & credit cards. American menu specializing in turkey & pie.

Exit 208 *continued*

Fast Food

③ **DENNY'S**

Lodging

⑥ **ARLINGTON MOTOR INN** ☺☺
$$ (206) 652-9595   Cash &
credit cards. Discounts avail-
able. Handicapped & non-
smoking rooms available, some
with refrigerators. Phones,
cable TV. Pets OK with fee.
Year-round spa. Coffee served
in lobby. Fax available. Truck
parking available.

Other

⑩ **FIRE STATION**

Exit 210

There are no services at this exit, but it's a good place to turn around!

Key Features: No services

Towing:
Plaza Towing 652-8488
Brandt's Towing 653-6454

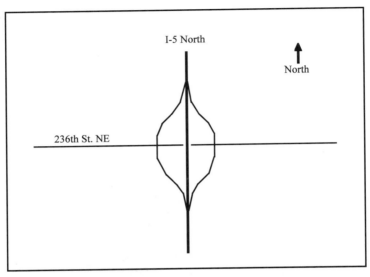

236th St. NE

I-5 North

North

No Services

Exit 212

This exit leads to Camano Island State Park, via WA 532 (19 miles from exit). Near the exit, you can get gas and a cup of espresso to wake you up.

Key Features: Camano Island State Park, gas

Towing: Plaza Towing 435-2361 (Arlington), 652-8488 (Stanwood)

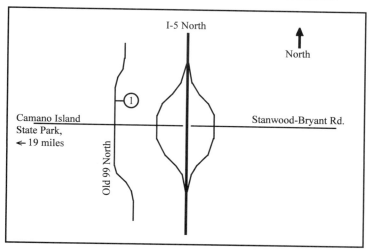

Service Stations

① **TEXACO**   4:30am-11pm. Self-serve, large mini-mart, cash & credit cards, diesel, propane, phone, espresso, ice.

Exit 215

This exit provides gas, a mini-mart, and a phone. A mechanic is available Tuesday-Saturday.

Key Features: Gas

Towing: C's Towing
629-3443 (Stanwood)

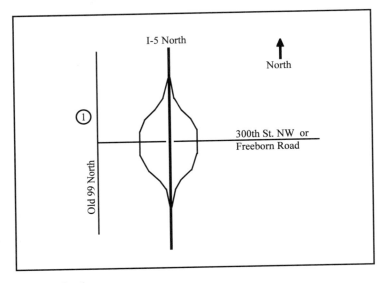

I-5 North

↑
North

300th St. NW or
Freeborn Road

Old 99 North

Service Stations

① **GAS MINI MART** 6am-8pm Mon-Fri, 7am-8pm Sat, 8am-8pm Sun. Self-serve, mini-mart, cash & credit cards, propane, phone. Mechanic available: Stuart's Freeborn Service 9am-5pm Tues-Sat, closed Sun & Mon, phone: 629-3443.

Exit 218

This exit provides accommodations in a very peaceful setting.

Key Features: Lodging

Towing:
Mt. Vernon Towing 336-3535

Exit 218

Starbird Rd.

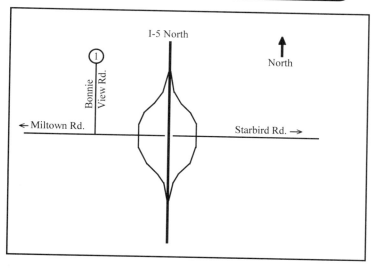

Lodging

① **HILLSIDE MOTEL** ☺ $$
(206) 445-3252 Cash & credit
cards. Weekly rates available.
Some kitchenettes, TV. Pets
OK with fee. Two units have
two bedrooms, each. Quiet,
peaceful setting.

Exit 221

This exit provides access to La Conner and Camano Island State Park, both some distance from the exit. Near the exit, you can get gas or diesel around the clock and there is a fire station, in case of emergency.

Key Features: 24-Hr. gas

Towing: Mount Vernon Towing 336-3535

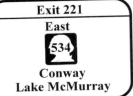

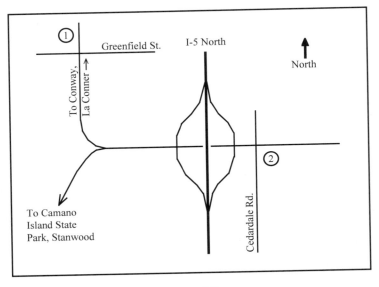

Service Stations

② **TEXACO** 24 Hrs.
Self-serve, mini-mart, cash & credit cards, diesel, restrooms, phone.

Other

① **CONWAY FIRE STATION**

This area is world-famous for its tulip farms. In the Spring, the tulip farms sport brilliant colors that stretch as far as the eye can see in every direction. Tourists flock to the area to see the tulips and order bulbs for their gardens.

Exit 224

This is a *Northbound* exit only. Southbound access is from Exit 225. Truck City and Cedardale Fire Station are midway between the two exits on Old Hwy 99. See Exit 225 for more information.

Key Features: See Exit 225

Towing: Mt. Vernon Towing 336-3535

> **Exit 224**
>
> **S. Mount Vernon**

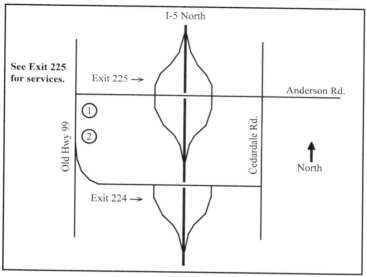

See Exit 225 for services.

I-5 North

Exit 225 →

Exit 224 →

Anderson Rd.

Old Hwy 99

Cedardale Rd.

① ②

North

Windmill at the RoozenGaarde Tulip Gardens.

Exit 225

This exit provides access to the south end of Mt. Vernon. (Exit 224 is also shown for reference.)

Key Features: Food and gas

Towing:
Mt. Vernon Towing 336-3535

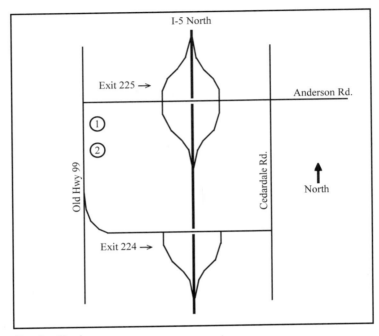

Service Stations

② **TRUCK CITY TRUCK STOP**
(EXXON)   24 Hrs.
Self- & full-serve, mini-mart, cash & credit cards, diesel, restrooms, phone. CB sales & repair.

Restaurants

② **TRUCK CITY TRUCK STOP** $$
(Crane's Restaurant) 24 Hrs.
Full & counter service with take-out available. Cash & credit cards. American menu. Full bar. Good food. No non-smoking area in restaurant.

Other

① **CEDARDALE FIRE STATION**

Exit 226

This exit leads to Mount Vernon city center and the Skagit Valley Hospital.

Key Features: Hospital

Towing:
Mt. Vernon Towing 336-3535,
Peter's Westside Towing 336-5312

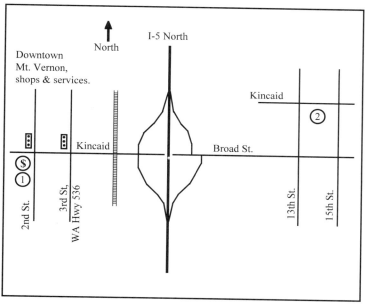

Other

① **RED APPLE MARKET**
  • 6am-12pm
  • Accepts credit cards

② **SKAGIT VALLEY HOSPITAL**

Exit 227

This exit has something for everyone, with numerous restaurants, service stations, and motels to suit every budget.

Key Features: Food, gas, lodging

Towing:
Mt. Vernon Towing 336-3535
Skagit Valley Towing 757-4774

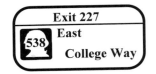

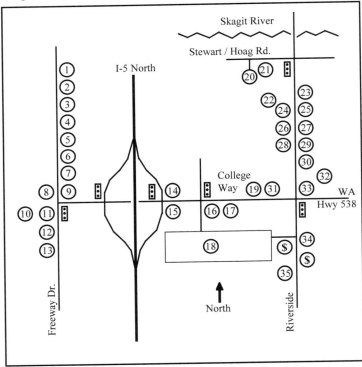

Service Stations

⑨ **CHEVRON**   24 Hrs.
Self-serve, mini-mart, cash & credit cards, diesel, handicapped-access restrooms, phone. Drive-thru car wash open 7am-7pm Mon-Thu, 7am-8pm Fri-Sat, 8am-6pm Sun.

⑬ **TEXACO**   6am-10pm
Mon-Sat, 7am-10pm Sun. Self-serve, mini-mart, cash & credit cards, diesel, restrooms, phone.

⑯ **UNOCAL 76**   24 Hrs.
Self- and full-serve, cash & credit cards & checks, diesel, propane, restrooms, phone, ice. Mechanic on duty 8am-5pm Mon-Fri for major repairs; assistance available for minor repairs at other times.

㉝ **EXXON**   7am-10pm
Mon-Sat, 7am-9pm Sun. Self-serve, cash & credit cards.

Restaurants

③ **CRANBERRY TREE** $$$
Breakfast: 8am Sat-Sun. Lunch:
11am-4pm Mon-Sat. Dinner:
4pm-10pm Mon-Sat, 12pm-
10pm Sun. Full-service
restaurant. Cash & credit cards.
American menu. Full bar.
Reservations recommended:
424-7755.

⑦ **DRUMMAN'S** $$
5:30am-10pm Sun-Thurs,
5:30am-12am Fri-Sat. Full &
counter service available. Cash
& credit cards. American menu.

⑪ **MITZEL'S** $$
10am-10pm Sun-Thurs, 10am-
11pm Fri-Sat. Full & counter
service. Cash & credit cards.
American menu specializing in
pies & roast turkey. Beer &
wine available.

⑫ **PEKING** $$
11:30am-10pm Tues-Thurs,
11:30am-12am Fri, 12pm-12am
Sat, 4pm-10pm Sun, closed
Mon. Full & counter service
with take-out available. Cash &
credit cards & checks. Chinese
menu. Full bar.

㉑ **AUSTIN'S RIO CAFE** $$
7am-9pm Sun-Thurs, 7am-
11pm Fri-Sat. Full-service
restaurant. Cash & credit cards.
American menu featuring ribs
in a Western motif. Full bar.

㉒ **DRAGON INN** $$
11:30am-11pm Mon-Thurs,
11:30am-12am Fri, 12pm-12am
Sat, 12pm-10pm Sun. Full-
service restaurant. Cash & credit
cards. Chinese menu. Full bar.

㉓ **MAX DALE'S** $$
11am-10pm Mon-Thurs, 11am-
11pm Fri, 4pm-11pm Sat, 4pm-
9:30pm Sun. Full-service
restaurant. Cash & credit cards.
American menu. Full bar.

㉖ **CASCADE PIZZA INN** $$
11am-2am Mon-Sat, 12pm-
12am Sun. Full-service restaurant. Take-out available. Cash
& credit cards. Italian menu
specializing in pizza, chicken,
& ribs. Full bar.

Fast Food

① **ROYAL FORK BUFFET**
⑤ **ARBY'S**
⑥ **BURGER KING**
⑧ **DAIRY QUEEN**
⑭ **ROUND TABLE PIZZA**
⑮ **DENNY'S**
⑰ **JACK IN THE BOX**
⑲ **SKIPPER'S**
㉗ **MCDONALD'S**
㉘ **TACO BELL**
㉙ **SHAKEY'S**
㉚ **WINCHELL'S**
㉛ **BIG SCOOP**
㉞ **KENTUCKY FRIED CHICKEN**
㉟ **GODFATHER'S PIZZA**

Lodging

② **TULIP INN** ☺☺ $$
(206) 428-5969 Cash & credit
cards. Discounts & weekly rates
available. Handicapped & non-
smoking rooms available. Some
kitchenettes, phones, cable TV.
Pets OK with fee. Fax avail-
able.

Exit 227 *continued*

④ **TRAVELODGE** ☺☺☺ $$$
(206) 428-7020 Handicapped &
non-smoking rooms available.
Cash & credit cards & checks.
Discounts & weekly rates
available. Some rooms with
kitchenettes, some with
refrigerators. Honeymoon suite
& some family suites. Phones,
cable TV, elevators, indoor
heated pool & spa. Guest
laundry, fax. Continental
breakfast served in office.
Coffee with *USA Today*
newspaper provided in each
room. Pets OK with fee.

⑩ **BEST WESTERN MOTOR INN**
(206) 424-4287 ☺☺☺ $$$
Non-smoking rooms available.
Some rooms have kitchenettes
or refrigerators. Some family
suites. Many rooms have
balcony overlooking pool. Cash
& credit cards. Discounts &
weekly rates available. Phones,
cable TV, spa, outdoor seasonal
pool. Pets OK with fee. Phones
for the hearing-impaired
available. Meeting room, fax.
Large truck parking area.
Coffee available in rooms & in
lobby.

⑳ **COTTONTREE INN** $$$
Reviewers not permitted to see
rooms. (206) 428-5678
Handicapped & non-smoking
rooms available. Some family
suites. Refrigerators
available on request. Cash &
credit cards & checks. Discounts
& weekly rates available.
Phones, cable TV, outdoor
seasonal pool. Pets OK. VCR &
tape rental available. Sea-Tac-
Bellingham Airporter stops
here. Next door to Riverside
Health Club.

㉔ **TOWNE AND COUNTRY MOTOR
INN** 1-800-882-4141 ☺☺ $$$
Local: (206) 424-4141 Non-
smoking rooms available. Cash
& credit cards. Discounts
available. Phones, cable TV,
elevators, spa, outdoor seasonal
pool. Pets OK with fee.
Attached restaurant: Skagit
Valley Steak House & Lounge,
Full bar.

㉕ **WEST WINDS MOTEL** ☺ $$
(206) 424-4224 Non-smoking
rooms available. Some rooms
have refrigerators. Cash &
credit cards. Discounts &
weekly rates available. Phones,
cable TV. Pets OK with fee.
Coffee available in rooms.

Other

⑱ **SKAGIT VALLEY SQUARE**
- Ernst
- Starbucks Coffee
- Payless
- Albertson's
- Hallmark
- Craft Outlet
- Phone

㉜ **SAFEWAY**
- 24 Hrs.
- Phone
- Pharmacy

Truck caught well under the speed limit!

Exit 229

This exit provides access to wonderful shopping at the Cascade Mall, Cascade Plaza, and Pacific Edge Outlet Center.

Key Features: Shopping

Towing:
Burlington Towing 757-8697, Skagit Valley Towing 757-4774

Northbound:

> **Exit 229**
>
> **George Hopper Rd.**

Southbound:

> **Exit 229**
>
> **George Hopper Road**

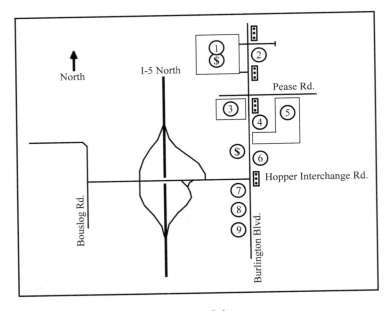

I-5 North

North

Pease Rd.

Hopper Interchange Rd.

Bouslog Rd.

Burlington Blvd.

Service Stations

② **CENEX GAS**   7am-7pm (commercial fueling 24 Hrs.) Self- & full-serve, cash & credit cards, diesel, phone.

⑦ **USA MINI MART**   24 Hrs. Self-serve, mini-mart, cash & credit cards & checks, diesel, restrooms, phone.

Fast Food

① **BURGER KING**
④ **WENDY'S**

Other

① **CASCADE MALL**
  • Sears with Auto Center
  • Emporium
  • J.C. Penney
  • Bon Marche
  • Target
  • Burger King
  • Red Robin
  • Many smaller shops & eating establishments

③ **PACIFIC EDGE OUTLET CENTER**
- Liz Claiborne
- Corning Revere
- Toys Unlimited
- Shoe Pavilion
- Public restrooms
- Phones
- Many other shops

⑤ **CASCADE PLAZA**
- Picway Shoes
- Discount Clothing
- K-Mart
- Food Pavilion (24 Hrs.)
- Soap Opera Laundry
- Sub Shop
- Teriyaki Bowl
- Phones

⑥ **SKAGIT ANIMAL CLINIC**

⑧ **PETS R US**

⑨ **PENNZOIL 10 MIN LUBE**
- 8am-6pm Mon-Sat

Ark-shaped "Children's Church" near the Cascade Mall, Exit 229.

Exit 230

This exit features numerous motels, restaurants, and 24-Hr. services. You also take this exit to reach the North Cascades Highway, the Whidbey Island - San Juan Ferry, and tourist attractions around the town of La Conner. See Exit 231 for additional services available northbound on Burlington Blvd.

Key Features: Whidbey Island - San Juan Ferry, 24-hour gas, food and lodging.

Towing: Skagit Valley Towing 757-4774; Burlington Towing 757-8697

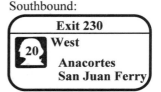

Northbound:

Exit 230
20 Burlington Anacortes

Southbound:

Exit 230
20 West Anacortes San Juan Ferry

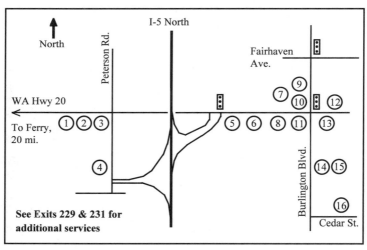

Service Stations

① **Holiday Market / Chevron** 24 Hrs. Self-serve, grocery store, cash & credit cards, diesel, restrooms, ice, phone. Boating, camping, & fishing supplies, fresh doughnuts.

② **Arco am/pm** 24 Hrs. Self-serve, cash & cash-machine cards, restroom, ice, phones.

⑩ **Texaco** Being remodeled when reviewed.

⑪ **Exxon** 24 Hrs. Self-serve, mini-mart, cash & credit cards & checks, restrooms, phone.

Restaurants

⑤ **The Galley** $$ 6am-9:30pm 7 days. Full & counter service. Cash & credit cards & checks. Seafood & steak. Full bar.

Exit 230 *continued*

⑧ **ZACK'S** $$
8am-9pm Sun-Thur, 8am-10pm
Fri-Sat. Full service. Cash &
credit cards. Italian menu
specializing in seafood & steak.
Full bar.

⑨ **EL CAZADOR** $$
11am-10pm Mon-Thur, 11am-
11pm Fri-Sat, 10am-10pm Sun.
Full service. Cash & credit
cards. Mexican menu. Full bar.

⑮ **CHINA WOK** $$
11:30am-10pm Mon-Thur,
11:30am-10:30pm Fri-Sat, noon
-10pm Sun.   (206) 757-0074
Full service with take-out
available. Cash & credit cards.
Chinese menu. Full bar.

Fast Food

④ **MCDONALD'S**

⑫ **SAUCY'S PIZZA**

⑬ **JACK IN THE BOX**

⑯ **PIZZA FACTORY**

Lodging

③ **MARK II MOTEL** ☺ $$
(206) 757-4021 Non-smoking
rooms available, kitchenettes, &
refrigerators. Cash & credit
cards & checks. Phones, cable
TV. No wheelchair access.
Weekly rates available. Pets OK.

⑥ **COCUSA MOTEL** ☺☺ $$$
(206) 757-6044   Non-smoking
& handicapped rooms available,
some kitchenettes & refrigera-
tors. Cash & credit cards &
checks. Phones, cable TV. No
pets. Recliners in rooms, guest
laundry, bath tubs & showers,
coffee in lobby 24 hrs. Outdoor
seasonal pool & spa.

⑭ **STERLING MOTOR INN** ☺ $$$
1-800-338-3112 or (206) 757-0071
Non-smoking rooms available.
Some rooms have kitchenettes,
waterbeds. No wheelchair
access. Cash & credit cards &
company checks. Discounts &
weekly rates available. Phone,
cable TV. *Attached Restaurant:*
China Wok (reviewed
separately).

Other

⑦ **MAGIC CAR WASH**

Exit 231

This exit provides access to the town of Burlington, Chuckanut Drive (WA 11), or the North Cascades Hwy (WA 20). See Exit 230 for additional services available southbound on Burlington Blvd.

Key Features: Burlington, gas, and food.

Towing: Skagit Valley Towing 757-4774; Evergreen Chevron 755-0070

Northbound: Southbound:

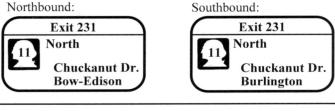

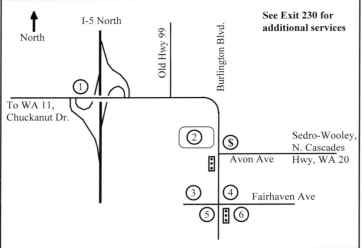

Service Stations

⑤ **CHEVRON** 24 Hrs. Self-serve, tiny mini-mart, cash & credit cards, restrooms, ice, phone, and propane. Mechanic on duty 8am-6pm Mon-Sat. Towing: 755-0070.

④ **BP** 6am-8pm Mon-Sat, 9am-8pm Sun. Self-serve, cash & credit cards, restrooms. Drive-thru car wash.

Other

① **WASHINGTON STATE PATROL**
② **CITY PARK**
 • Children's play area
③ **SKAGIT VALLEY TOWING**
 • 757-4774
⑥ **THRIFTY FOODS**
 • 7am-midnight, 7 days
 • Phones
 • Koren's Drug Store

Exit 232

This exit leads to the town of Sedro-Wooley and the North Cascades Highway (Hwy 20). Additional services are available south on Old Hwy 99 in Burlington.

Key Features: Phone

Towing:
Mt. Vernon Towing 336-3535
Bow Hill Towing 757-8697

Exit 232

**Cook Road
Sedro-Woolley**

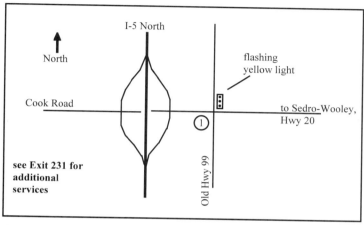

Other

① PHONE
   at the commercial fueling
   station.

Exit 236

This exit features two nice campgrounds, access to WA Hwy 99, Chuckanut Drive, and a convenient public phone.

Key Features: Camping and a phone

Towing: Skagit Valley Towing 757-4774

Northbound:

Exit 236
Bow Hill Road

Southbound:

Exit 236
Bow-Edison Bow Hill Rd.

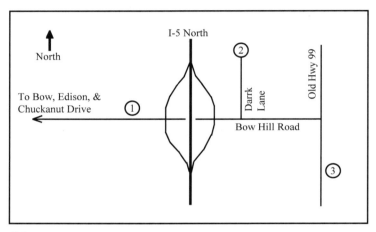

Other

① FISH MARKET / OUTLET
  • Public phone

② THOUSAND TRAILS CAMPGROUND
  • Seasonal - open summer
  • 1 mile from Bow Hill Rd.

③ KOA CAMPGROUND
  • Year-'round
  • Store: 9-11am & 4-6pm
  • Showers, laundry
  • Seasonal pool & sauna
  • Children's playground
  • Picnic area
  • Note: There is no sign pointing back to I-5. Watch for the Bow Hill Rd. sign.

Bow Hill Rest Area

Northbound: At mile-marker 238, the Bow Hill Rest Area features:

- Phones
- Handicapped restrooms
- Picnic areas
- Travel information

Southbound: At mile-marker 239, the Bow Hill Rest Area features:

- Phones
- Handicapped restrooms
- Picnic areas
- Travel information

Truck Weigh Station

Southbound: At mile-marker 236, the truck weigh station features phones and a mail box.

Bow Hill Rest Area in the wintertime.

Exit 240

This exit features gas in the town of Alger, on Old Highway 99.

Key Features: Gas

Towing:
Skagit Valley Towing 757-4774

> **Exit 240**
>
> **Alger**

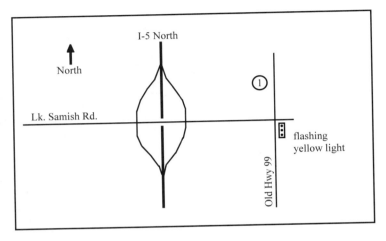

Service Stations

① **ALGER PIT STOP** 7am-6pm, 7 days (206)724-5503 Full-serve with mini-mart. Cash & credit cards, restrooms, limited wheelchair access, phones.

Exit 242

There are no services available at this exit.

Key Features: No services.

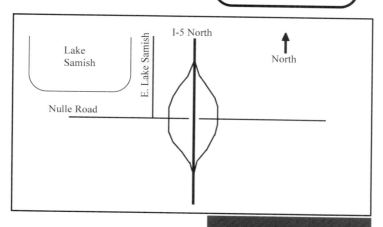

Exit 242

Nulle Rd.
So. Lake Samish

Lake Samish

E. Lake Samish

I-5 North

North

Nulle Road

Even smokestacks can be interesting...

Exit 246

This exit provides access to Lake Samish, along with gas and a mini-mart.

Key Features: Lake Samish

Towing:
Johnson's Towing 733-4232
Berk's Towing 734-4738

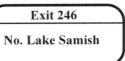

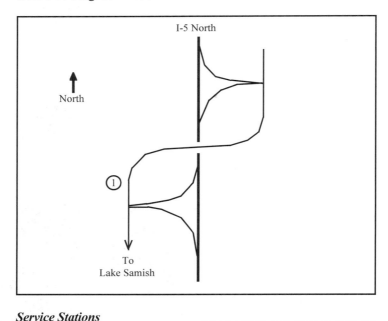

Service Stations

① TEXACO   7:30am-7pm
Mon-Sat, 8:30am-7pm Sun.
Self-serve with mini-mart. Cash
& credit cards, no restroom,
phones, ice.

Exit 250

This exit offers auto services near the exit, as well as access to the Alaska Ferry, Larrabee State Park, Chuckanut Bay, and the town of Fairhaven, all to the west.

Key Features: Alaska Ferry, Fairhaven.

Towing:
Horton's Towing 733-1230
Johnson's Towing 733-4232

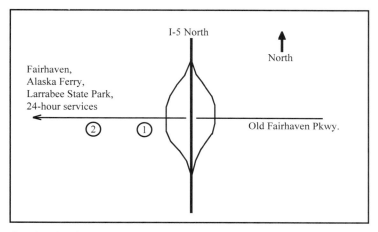

Service Stations

① **CHEVRON**   7am-10pm, 7 days. Self- & partial-serve, cash & credit cards, restrooms, phones, propane, and ice. Mechanic available 8am-4pm, 7 days.

Other

② **FAIRHAVEN VETERINARY HOSPITAL**

Exit 252

This exit features many good motels, access to Western Washington University, and a wide variety of restaurants.

Key Features: Western Washington University

Towing:
Horton's Towing 733-1230
Johnson's Towing 733-4232

> **Exit 252**
>
> **Samish Way**
> **W. Wash. University**

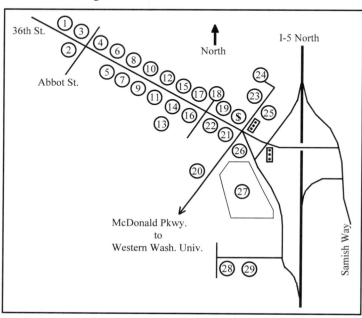

Service Stations

(17) **CHEVRON**   7am-11pm
Mon-Thur, 7am-12am Fri-Sat,
7am-10pm Sun. 676-0980 Self-
& full-serve, mini-mart, ice,
cash & credit cards, restrooms,
phone, towing. Mechanic on
duty 8am-6pm 7 days.

(19) **ARCO AM/PM**   24 Hrs.
Self-serve, mini-mart, cash &
cash-machine cards, restrooms,
phone.

(22) **TEXACO** 6am-12am, 7 days.
Self-serve, small mini-mart.
Cash & credit cards, restrooms,
phones, diesel.

(26) **UNOCAL 76**   7am-10am,
7 days. Self- & full-serve, tiny
mini-mart. Cash & credit cards,
restrooms, phones, ice, and
propane. Mechanic on duty
8am-5pm Mon-Fri.

(28) **STARVIN SAM'S BP &
MINI-MART** 7am-11pm, Sun-
Thur, 7am-2am Fri-Sat. Self-
serve, large mini-mart. Cash &
credit cards, phones, restrooms
with handicapped access.

Exit 252 *continued*

Restaurants

③ **RIB N' BEEF** $$
7am-10pm, 7 days. Full service. Cash & credit cards & checks. Greek menu, specializing in seafood & steak. Full bar.

⑦ **FRYDAY'S** $$
11am-11pm, 7 days. Full service with take-out available. Cash & credit cards & checks. American menu specializing in burgers & old-fashioned milkshakes with ice cream, milk, & lots of flavors. Atmosphere is 50's nostalgia with good food. Full bar.

⑮ **SMILEY'S PIZZA** $$
11am-10pm Sun-Thur, 11am-11pm Fri-Sat 733-4880 Full service, counter, take-out & delivery available. Cash & credit cards & checks. Italian menu specializing in pizza. Full bar.

⑱ **BLACK ANGUS** $$
11am-10pm Mon-Thur, 11am-11pm Fri-Sat, noon-10pm Sun. Full service with take-out available. Cash & credit cards. American menu specializing in good steak & seafood. Full bar.

⑳ **BAMBOO INN** $$
11:30am-2pm Tues-Fri for lunch, dinners: 4pm-10pm Tues-Thur, 4pm-11pm Fri-Sat, noon-9pm Sun. Full service. Cash & credit cards. Chinese menu. Beer & wine.

㉓ **CALICO INN PANCAKE HOUSE** $$ 6am-10pm, 7 days. Counter & full service. Cash & credit cards & local checks. American menu. No wheelchair access.

㉙ **THE KEG** $$
11:30am-10pm Mon-Thur, 11:30am-11pm Fri, 4pm-11pm Sat, 2pm-9:30pm Sun. 738-0275 Full service. Cash & credit cards. American menu specializing in steak and seafood. Full bar.

Fast Food

④ **BOOMER'S DRIVE-INN BURGERS**
⑨ **McDONALD'S**
⑪ **ARBY'S**
⑬ **SUBWAY**
⑭ **GODFATHER'S PIZZA**
㉑ **BURGER KING**
㉕ **DENNY'S**
㉗ **ROUND TABLE PIZZA**
㉗ **QUARTERBACK PUB & EATERY**

Lodging

① **MAC'S MOTEL** ☺ $$
(206) 734-7570 7am-11pm. All smoking rooms. Wheelchair access to 1st floor. Cash & credit cards. Phones, cable TV. Pets welcome with no fee. Coffee in office.

② **ALOHA MOTEL** ☺☺ $$
(206) 733-4900 Non-smoking rooms available. Cash & credit cards. Discounts for seniors. Phones, cable TV. No pets. Kitchenettes, refrigerators, & family suites available. Picnic area, small Japanese garden & park. Very attractive. Continental breakfast in office.

_____

_____

_____

_____

Exit 252 *continued*

⑤ **RAMADA INN** ☺☺ $$$
1-800-272-6232 or (206)734-8830
Non-smoking rooms available,
all with refrigerators. Cash &
credit cards & non-local checks.
Phone, cable TV, seasonal
outdoor pool. Continental
breakfast included.

⑥ **KEY MOTEL** ☺☺ $$
(winter) $$$ (summer) (206)
733-4060 Non-smoking rooms.
Some refrigerators available,
two family suites. No wheel-
chair access. Cash & credit
cards. Discounts available.
Phone, cable TV, spa, outdoor
seasonal pool. No pets. Coffee
in office.

⑧ **BELL NORTHWOODS MOTEL**
(206) 733-2520 ☺☺ $$
Non-smoking rooms, most with
kitchenettes. Cash & credit
cards. Discounts for seniors in
the summer. Cable TV, phone,
picnic area with B-B-Q. Pets
OK with fee. Many family
suites for 2, 4, or 8.

⑩ **COACHMAN INN** ☺☺ $$
1-800-962-6641 or (206) 671-9000
Non-smoking rooms, some with
refrigerators. One kitchenette
available. Cash & credit cards.
Cable TV, phone, outdoor
seasonal pool, sauna, jacuzzi.
No pets. Continental breakfast
in lobby. *Families:* check to see
if the manager's suite is
available.

⑫ **BAY CITY MOTOR INN**
1-800-538-8204 ☺☺☺ $$$
or (206) 676-0332. Non-
smoking & handicapped rooms
available. Some rooms have
refrigerators & there is one
kitchenette. Cash & credit cards.
Cable TV, phone, elevators.
Exercise area with pool table.
Some rooms have jacuzzis. No
pets. Continental breakfast in
lobby, with snacks all day.

⑯ **PARK MOTEL** ☺☺☺ $$$
1-800-732-1225 or (206) 733-8280
Non-smoking & handicapped
rooms (with closed-caption
TV's). Refrigerators on request,
one kitchenette available, one
apt. for families. Cash & credit
cards. Cable TV, phone, sauna,
& jacuzzi. No pets. Continental
breakfast in lobby, with coffee
& snacks all day. Fax, copy
machine. Shuttle service: motel
will pay one way of a local taxi
ride.

㉔ **MOTEL 6** Reviewers
not permitted to see rooms. $$
(206) 671-4494 Non-smoking
rooms available. Cash & credit
cards. Cable TV, phone, outdoor
seasonal pool. Handicapped
access to first floor.

Other

㉗ **SEHOME VILLAGE MALL**
  • Haggen market &
       restaurant (24 Hrs)
       Cash-machine inside.
  • Payless Drugs
  • Round Table Pizza
  • Quarterback Pub &
       Eatery
  • Starbucks Coffee
  • The Bagel Factory
  • The Children's Co.
  • Pet Stop
  • Phone

Bellingham (population approximately 52,000) is located in Whatcom County, the most northwesterly county in the U.S. "Whatcom" was originally the name of a creek, from an Indian word meaning "noisy all the time." Bellingham overlooks Bellingham Bay and the San Juan Islands.

Western Washington University (9,000 students) is located near Exit 252. Founded in 1893, it has been a regional university since 1977.

If you have a little extra time, stop to walk through one of the interesting historic areas in downtown Bellingham or through the outdoor sculpture museum located on the W.W.U. campus.

Exit 253

This exit provides access to Bellingham city center (west on Lakeway Drive), St. Joseph's Hospital, and a Visitor Information Center, along with restaurants, motels, and service stations.

Key Features: Bellingham city center

Towing:
Berk's Towing 734-4738
Horton's Towing 733-1230

Exit 253

Lakeway Dr.

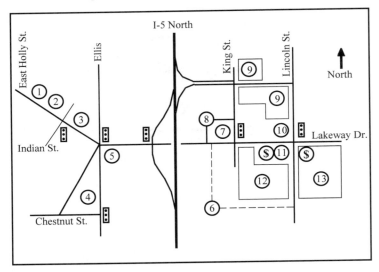

Service Stations

⑤ **TEXACO**
Under construction.

⑪ **DISCOUNT TIRE CO. (USA GASOLINE)**   24 Hrs.
Self-serve, small mini-mart, cash only, no restrooms, no phone. Tire store open 8:30am-6pm Mon-Fri, 8:30am-5pm Sat, closed Sun. Credit cards OK for tire service.

Restaurants

⑩ **SADIGHI'S** $$$
Opens 5pm for dinner Mon-Fri, 4:30pm Sat-Sun, closed Tuesdays. (206) 647-1109. Cash & credit cards. Full-service restaurant featuring steak & seafood. Full bar.

Fast Food

② **BASKIN-ROBBINS**
③ **TACO TIME**
⑦ **PIZZA HUT**
⑬ **LITTLE CAESAR'S PIZZA**

Lodging

① **SHANGRI-LA MOTEL** ☺ $$
(206) 733-7050 Cash & credit cards. Weekly rates available. Some kitchenettes, some refrigerators, phones, cable TV. Pets OK with fee. Coffee in the office.

⑥ **BEST WESTERN LAKEWAY INN**
☺☺☺ $$$ 1-800-528-1234,
local: 671-1011. Non-smoking &
handicapped rooms available.
Cash & credit cards & checks.
Discounts available. Phones,
cable TV, elevators, "Full-service
hotel." Some suites. No pets.
Some rooms open onto pool area.
Indoor pool, spa, exercise room,
tanning bed, hair salon. Shuttle
service to airport, bus, ferry
terminal, & local shopping.
Attached restaurant: Harry O's,
$$, full bar.

⑧ **VAL-U INN MOTEL** ☺☺ $$$
1-800-443-7777, local: 671-9600
Non-smoking & handicapped
rooms available. Some rooms
have refrigerators. Cash & credit
cards & checks with guaranty
card. Discounts & weekly rates
available. Phones, waterbeds,
cable TV, elevators. Pets OK
with fee. Guest laundry, spa,
VCR rentals with movies, food
vending machines. Shuttle
service to airport, bus, & ferry
terminal. Continental breakfast
served in lobby eating area.

Other

④ **ST. JOSEPH'S HOSPITAL**
  • South Campus

⑨ **DISCOVERY PARK MALL**
  • Ricky's Restaurant
  • R.E.freshers
  • Antiques, Books
  • Postal Place (copies, fax)
  • Phone
  • Bergsma Gallery & Cafe
  • Visitor Information Center
      8:30am-5:30pm, 7 days
      handicapped restrooms

⑫ **FRED MEYER**
  • 7am-11pm, 7 days

⑬ **LAKEWAY CENTER**
  • Ennen's Foods (24 hrs.)
  • Little Caesar's Pizza
  • Eleni's Greek Restaurant
  • Seattle Film Works
  • Coin-op laundry & dry
      cleaning

Exit 254

This exit provides access to the goods and services located near State, Iowa, and Ohio Streets in Bellingham. You can grab a quick bite to eat or buy gas at this exit.

Key Features: Fast food and gas

Towing: Horton's Towing 733-1230, Johnson's Towing 733-4232

Northbound:

Exit 254
State St.
Iowa St.

Southbound:

Exit 254
State St.
Ohio St.

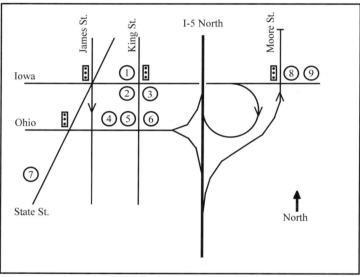

Service Stations

③ **CHEVRON**   24 Hrs.
Self- & full-serve, mini-mart, cash & credit cards, propane, RV pump-out, ice, restrooms, phone.

⑤ **UNOCAL 76**   24 Hrs.
Self- & full-serve, small mini-mart, cash & credit cards, RV pump-out, propane, ice, restrooms. Mechanic on duty 8am-5pm Mon-Fri, 8am-4:30pm Sat.

⑧ **BP**   24 Hrs.
Self-serve, mini-mart, cash & credit cards, restrooms, phone.

⑨ **TEXACO**   7am-10pm, 7 days. Self-serve, small mini-mart, cash & credit cards, propane, restrooms, phone.

Fast Food

① **DAIRY QUEEN**
⑥ **McDONALD'S**
⑦ **SKIPPER'S**

Other

② **JALOPY JAKOOZEE CAR WASH**
④ **FOREIGN AUTO REPAIR**

Exit 255

This exit provides access to shopping at the Sunset Square Mall, as well as food and gas.

Key Features: Sunset Square Mall

Towing:
Berk's Towing 734-4738
Horton's Towing 733-1230

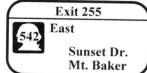

Exit 255
542 **East**

**Sunset Dr.
Mt. Baker**

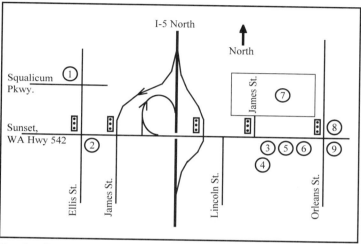

Service Stations

② **BP**　　　6am-10pm
Mon-Fri, 8am-11pm Sat, 9am-10pm Sun. Self-serve, mini-mart with fresh donuts daily, cash & credit cards, phone.

⑤ **CLASSIC GAS**　24 Hrs.
Self-serve, cash & credit cards & checks, diesel, no phone.

⑧ **SUNSET SELF-SERVE GAS**
6am-12 am, 7 days. Self-serve, cash & credit cards, phone.

⑨ **JACKPOT FOOD MART (& GAS)** 6am-11pm Mon-Sat, 6am-10pm Sun. Self-serve, mini-mart, cash & credit cards, phone.

Fast Food

③ **SUNSET BURGERS**

Other

① **ST. JOSEPH HOSPITAL**

④ **SUNSET CAR WASH**

⑥ **7-11**　(phone)

⑦ **SUNSET SQUARE MALL**
- The Fair (24 Hrs. food)
- Payless Drug
- Mail Boxes, etc.
- Pets-R-Us
- Maytag Laundry
- North China Restaurant
- TCBY Yogurt
- Round Table Pizza
- Taco Bell
- Jack in the Box
- Starbucks Coffee
- Slo-Pitch Pub & Eatery
- White Spot Restaurant
- Port of Subs
- Winchell's Eatery
- Cinemas
- Pacific Linen
- K-mart,　phone
- Numerous other shops

Exit 256

This exit features abundant shopping at the Bellis Fair Mall and the surrounding area.

Key Features: Bellis Fair Mall

Towing:
Johnson's Towing 733-4232
Berk's Towing 734-4738

Southbound:

Exit 256
539 **North**
Meridian St.
Bellis Fair-
Mall Pkwy.

Northbound:

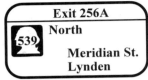

Exit 256A
539 **North**
Meridian St.
Lynden

Exit 256B
Bellis Fair-
Mall Pkwy.

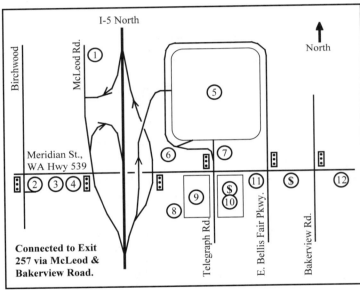

Connected to Exit 257 via McLeod & Bakerview Road.

Service Stations

⑪ **TEXACO**   24 Hrs.
Self-serve, mini-mart, cash & credit cards, diesel, handicapped restrooms, phone, cash machine.

⑫ **UNOCAL 76** 6:30am-10pm.
Self-serve, mini-mart, cash & credit cards & checks, diesel, no restrooms, no phone. Drive-thru car wash open 8am-8pm Mon-Sat, 9am-7pm Sun.

Restaurants

③ **CALICO FAMILY RESTAURANT**
$$ 6am-12am 7 days. Full- & counter service. Take-out available. Cash & credit cards. American menu specializing in home-made pies.

⑦ **RED ROBIN** $$$
11am-2am Mon-Sat, 9am-2am Sun. Cash & credit cards. Full-service restaurant featuring excellent burgers & a Sunday brunch. Full bar.

Exit 256 *continued*

Fast Food

- ⑥ MᴄDᴏɴᴀʟᴅ'ꜱ
- ⑦ Tᴀᴄᴏ Tɪᴍᴇ
- ⑨ Bᴜʀɢᴇʀ Kɪɴɢ
- ⑨ Dᴇɴɴʏ'ꜱ
- ⑨ Gᴏᴅꜰᴀᴛʜᴇʀ'ꜱ Pɪᴢᴢᴀ

Lodging

② CᴀɴAᴍ Iɴɴ ☺☺☺ $$$
(206) 738-6000 or 1-800-688-8030
Cash & credit cards & checks.
Discounts available. Canadian
currency taken at par. Handi-
capped & non-smoking rooms
available. Elevators, phones,
cable TV. Pets OK with fee.
Spa. Guest laundry. Shuttle
service to airport and bus
terminal.

④ Tʀᴀᴠᴇʟᴇʀꜱ Iɴɴ $$$
Reviewers not permitted to see
rooms. (206) 671-4600 Cash &
credit cards. Discounts available. Handicapped & non-
smoking rooms available. Some
rooms with refrigerators.
Elevators, phones, cable TV.
Small pets OK with fee.
Outdoor seasonal pool, spa.
Guest laundry. Coffee in lobby.

⑧ Bᴇꜱᴛ Wᴇꜱᴛᴇʀɴ Hᴇʀɪᴛᴀɢᴇ Iɴɴ
1-800-528-1234 ☺☺☺ $$$
local: 647-1912 Rooms have
antique theme, with lovely
cherry-wood furniture. Some
rooms have raised 4-poster beds.
Non-smoking & handicapped
rooms available. Many rooms
have kitchenettes. Cash &
credit cards & checks. Dis-
counts available. Phones, cable

TV. No pets. Outdoor seasonal
pool, year-'round spa, laundry
& same-day dry cleaning. Limo
service to airport, bus, Alaska
Ferry. Passes to local athletic
club available. Extensive
continental breakfast served in
lobby. Coffee in rooms.

Other

① Wᴀꜱʜɪɴɢᴛᴏɴ Sᴛᴀᴛᴇ Pᴀᴛʀᴏʟ

⑤ Bᴇʟʟɪꜱ Fᴀɪʀ Mᴀʟʟ
- Mervyn's
- Bon Marche
- Target
- Sears
- J.C. Penney
- Nordstrom
- Big 5
- Cinemas
- Food Court
- Many other stores

⑨ Mᴇʀɪᴅɪᴀɴ Pʟᴀᴢᴀ
- Denny's
- Burger King
- Mitzel's Restaurant
- Godfather's Pizza
- Mi Pueblo Mexican
  Restaurant
- Phone
- The Mail Room: Fax,
  Western Union, mail
  boxes

⑩ Mᴇʀɪᴅɪᴀɴ Vɪʟʟᴀɢᴇ
- Sizzler
- Shari's
- Mi Mexico Restaurant
- Payless Drug
- Ross
- Ernst
- Taco Time
- Taste of India Restaurant
- Bosley's Pet Food Mart
- Thai House Restaurant
- Phones
- Shoe Pavilion

Exit 257

There are no services at this exit. However, there is a fire station and an office of the US Border Patrol here, in case of emergency.

Key Features: No services

Towing:
Berks Towing 734-4738

> **Exit 257**
>
> **Northwest Ave.**

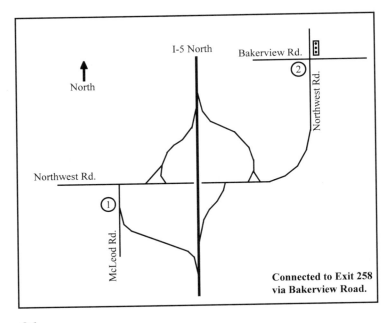

Connected to Exit 258 via Bakerview Road.

Other

① **US BORDER PATROL**

② **FIRE STATION**

Watch out for a cat at this exit!

Exit 258

This exit provides access to Bellingham International Airport, as well as accommodations and services.

Key Features: Bellingham International Airport

Towing:
Berks Towing 734-4738

Exit 258

**Bakerview Rd.
Bellingham Airport**

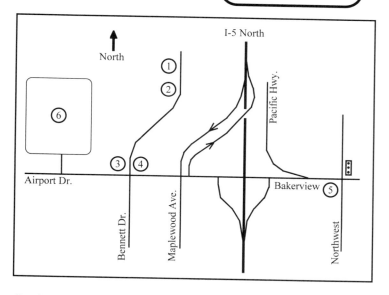

Service Stations

③ **BP**   24 Hrs.
Self-serve, mini-mart, cash & credit cards, restrooms, phone.

④ **EXXON**   24 Hrs.
Self-serve, mini-mart, cash & credit cards, diesel, restrooms, phone.

Lodging

① **SHAMROCK MOTEL** ☺ $$
(206) 676-1050 Cash & credit cards. Discounts available. Non-smoking & handicapped rooms available. Some kitchenettes, refrigerators in most rooms, phones, cable TV, guest laundry. Pets OK. Airport shuttle available. Coffee in the office.

② **HAMPTON INN** ☺☺☺ $$$
1-800-426-7866 or (206) 676-7700
Non-smoking rooms available. Cash & credit cards. Kids under 18 free in parents' room. Discounts available. Weekly rates available. Phones, cable TV. No pets. Outdoor heated pool. Exercise area & spa. Shuttle service to airport, nearby restaurants, & local shopping. Lavish continental breakfast served in lobby.

Other

⑤ **FIRE STATION**
⑥ **BELLINGHAM AIRPORT**
   • Greyhound Bus Terminal

The Lummi Indian Reservation (population approximately 3,000) is located West of Exit 260 on a peninsula fronting on the Straits of Georgia. The Lummi fishing fleet is the largest in the Northwest and Lummi smoked salmon is considered by many to be the best in the world.

Lummi Island is a long, mountainous island at the mouth of Bellingham Bay. It can only be reached by car ferry. It has a handful of permanent residents and there are several bed and breakfast inns to house overnight visitors.

Exit 260

This exit provides access to the Lummi Casino (10 miles from the exit) and the ferry to Lummi Island. Nearby, you can visit the I-5 Antique Mall.

Key Features: I-5 Antique Mall

Towing:
Horton's Towing 733-1230
Cascade Towing 384-6880

> **Exit 260**
>
> **Lummi Is.**
> **Slater Rd.**

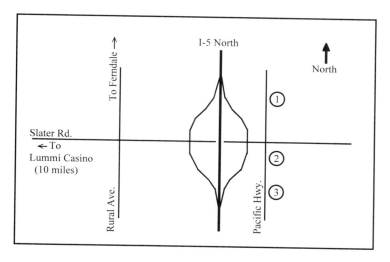

Service Stations

② **Arco am/pm**   24 hrs.
Self-serve, mini-mart, cash & cash machine cards, restrooms, phone.

Other

① **Ric's RV Outlet**
  • Propane
③ **I-5 Antique Mall**
  • Daily 10-5, Sunday 1-4

Exit 262

This exit leads to Ferndale city center, as well as a number of restaurants and other services.

Key Features: Ferndale city center, food & gas

Towing:
Cascade Towing 384-6880
Johnson's Towing 733-4232

> **Exit 262**
>
> **Main St.**
> **City Center**

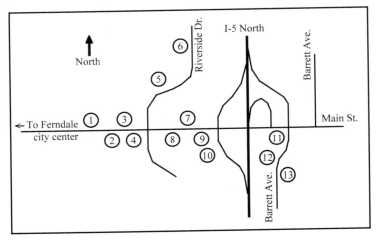

Service Stations

③ **EXXON**   5:30am-12:30am Mon-Thurs, 5:30am-1:00am Fri-Sat, 6:30am-12:30am Sun. Self-serve, mini-mart, cash & credit cards, restrooms, phone.

⑧ **TEXACO**   6am-12am 7 days. Self- & full-serve, mini-mart, cash & credit cards, diesel, propane, RV pump-out, phone, restrooms, ice. Mechanic on duty from 8am to 6pm, 7 days.

⑫ **BP**   7am-11pm 7 days. Self-serve, mini-mart, cash & credit cards, diesel, propane, phone.

Restaurants

④ **GREAT WALL** $$ Lunch: 11:30am-2:30am Mon-Fri, Dinner: 4pm-9pm Mon-Sat, closed Sun. Full-service restaurant. Take-out available. Cash & credit cards. Chinese menu.

⑨ **BOB'S BURGERS & BREW** $$ 7am-10pm Sun-Thurs, 7am-11pm Fri-Sat. Cash & credit cards & checks. Full-service restaurant featuring great burgers that taste like they just came off a grill in the back yard. Be sure to try the "Jo-Jo Fries" with your burger. Full bar.

⑪ SEA GALLEY $$
6am-10pm Mon-Thurs, 6am-11pm Fri-Sat, 8am-10pm Sun. Cash & credit cards. Full-service restaurant featuring seafood. Full bar.

Fast Food

② GRANT'S DRIVE-IN
   (old-fashioned drive-in)
⑤ DAIRY QUEEN

Lodging

⑥ SCOTTISH LODGE ☺☺ $$
(206) 384-4040 Cash & credit cards. Discounts available. Non-smoking rooms available. Some rooms have refrigerators. Phones, cable TV, outdoor seasonal pool. Pets OK with fee. Coffee available round the clock in the lobby; some food is for sale in lobby.

Other

① GLACIERVIEW ANIMAL HOSP.
⑦ VISITOR INFORMATION CENTER
⑩ SAVE-ON FOODS
   • 24 Hrs.
   • Phone
⑬ WHATCOM VETERINARY HOSPITAL
⑭ NORTHWEST PROPANE
   • 8:30am-4:30pm Mon-Fri

Exit 263

This exit leads to the Ferndale Campground.

Key Features:
Ferndale Campground, gas

Towing:
Cascade Towing 384-6880
Johnson's Towing 733-4232

> **Exit 263**
>
> **Portal Way**

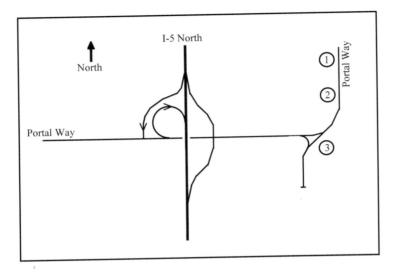

Service Stations

③ **TEXACO** 24 Hrs.
Self-serve, mini-mart, cash & credit cards & checks, diesel, restrooms, phone, kerosene.

② **PETE'S AUTO REPAIR** 7am-5:30pm Mon-Fri. AAA emergency service. NAPA Auto Care Center. Charge cards. Phone: 380-CARS.

Other

① **FERNDALE CAMPGROUND**
(Good Sam Park)
- 384-2622
- Groceries
- Laundromat
- Propane
- Game Room
- Phones
- Restrooms

Exit 266

This exit leads to Birch Bay, via WA Hwy 548. At the exit, there is a gas station and a fire station, in case of emergency.

Key Features: Gas

Towing: Cascade Towing 384-6880

Northbound: Southbound:

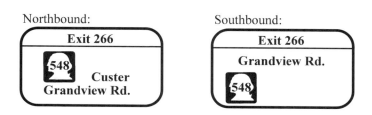

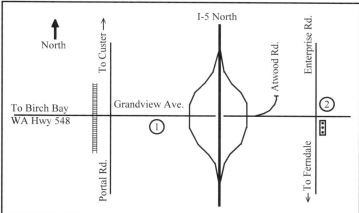

Service Stations

① **ARCO AM/PM**   24 Hrs.
Self-serve, mini-mart, cash & cash-machine cards, restrooms, phone.

Other

② **FIRE DEPARTMENT**

Custer Rest Area

Southbound: The Custer Rest Area at mile-marker 270
provides the following services:

- Picnic tables
- Handicapped restrooms
- Pet area
- Visitor Information Center
- Vending machines
- Free Coffee
- Potable water
- Phones

Northbound: At mile-marker 268, The Custer Rest Area
provides:

- Picnic tables
- Handicapped restrooms
- Pet area
- Travel Information
- Vending machines
- Free Coffee
- Potable water
- Phones

Exit 270

This exit specializes in Factory Outlet Shopping!

Key Features: Shopping, food

Towing: Cascade 384-6880

> **Exit 270**
> **Lynden**
> **Birch Bay**

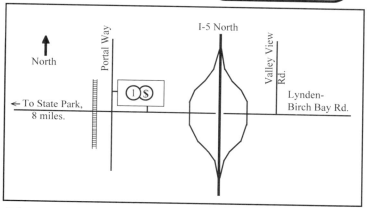

Other

(1) **PEACE ARCH FACTORY OUTLETS**
- Publisher's Warehouse
- Mikasa
- Van Heusen

- Corning Revere
- High Moon Cafe
- Levi's, Converse
- Geoffrey Beene
- 28 stores

Canadian and US flags fly side by side over businesses in this area, which also take either U.S. or Canadian currency. Photo: Exit 276.

Exit 274

This exit is a *Northbound* exit, only. There is no access Southbound. From this exit, you can reach Semiahmoo (5.6 miles), Birch Bay State Park (7 miles), and Blaine, via WA 548.

Key Features: AMMEX Duty Free & Windmill Pottery Shop

Towing: Cascade Towing 332-5626 or 384-6880

Exit 274

Peace Portal Dr. Semiahmoo

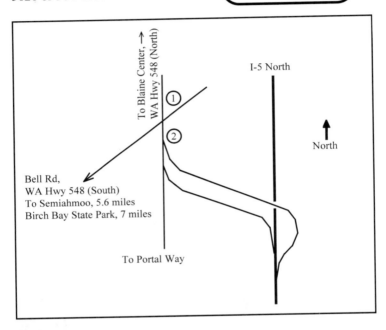

Service Stations

② SHELL 6am-12am 7 days. Self-serve, mini-mart, cash & credit cards, restrooms, phone.

Other

① AMMEX DUTY FREE & WINDMILL POTTERY SHOP
  • 8am-5pm Mon-Sat, 8am-7pm Sunday

Exit 275

This exit is a *Northbound* exit, only. All commercial vehicles must use this exit to enter Canada. Other vehicles can also use truck customs, if desired. Blaine Airport is located nearby.

Key Features: Truck customs, Blaine Airport, gas

Towing:
Cascade Towing 332-5626

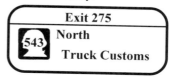

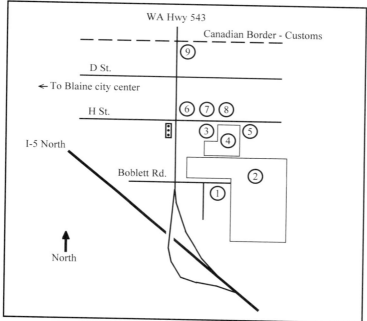

Service Stations

① **Exxon**   24 Hrs.
Self-serve, mini-mart, cash & credit cards, diesel, restrooms, phone.

③ **Texaco**   24 Hrs.
Self-serve, mini-mart, cash & credit cards, handicapped-access restrooms, diesel, drive-thru car wash, phone.

⑦ **BP**   24 Hrs.
Self-serve, large mini-mart, cash & credit cards, restrooms, phone.

⑨ **Ammex Duty Free** 24 Hrs.
Gas & diesel. If you come this far, you have to continue thru customs into Canada.

Fast Food

⑤ **Dairy Queen**
⑥ **Burger King**

Other

② **Blaine Airport**
④ **International Market Place Mall**
• Market Place Foods 24 Hrs.
• Payless Drugs
• Mail Boxes International
• Many other stores

⑧ **Border Patrol**

Exit 276

This exit provides access to Blaine city center and Peace Arch Park. It is the last Washington exit before the Canadian border if you're travelling North. If you're travelling South, welcome to Washington! Hope you'll enjoy your visit to our beautiful State!

Key Features: Blaine city center, Peace Arch Park

Towing: Bordertown Towing 332-4222, Berk's Towing 354-4415

Northbound:

> **Exit 276**
> **548** **South**
> **Blaine City Center**

Southbound:

> **Exit 276**
> **Blaine City Ctr.**
> **Peace Arch Park**
> **548** **Birch Bay**

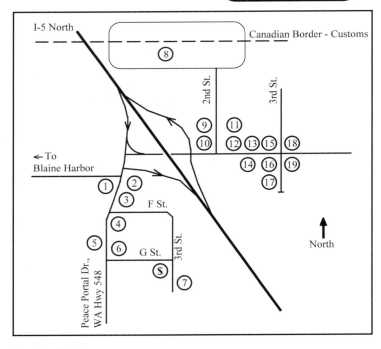

Service Stations

③ **SHELL** 6am-12am, 7days. Self-serve, mini-mart, cash & credit cards, restrooms.

④ **EXXON** 24 Hrs. Self-serve, large mini-mart serving hot food, cash & credit cards, drive-thru car wash, restrooms, phone, ice.

⑥ **CHEVRON** 24 Hrs. Self- & full-serve, mini-mart, cash & credit cards, ice.

⑪ **AMMEX DUTY-FREE SHOP** 7am-11pm, 7 days. Self-serve, duty-free shop, cash & credit cards, restrooms with handicapped access, phone.

Exit 276 *continued*

⑬ **Texaco** 24 Hrs.
Self-serve, cash & credit cards.

⑭ **Unocal 76 Gas** 24 Hrs.
Self-serve, tiny mini-mart, cash
& credit cards, restrooms,
phone.

⑯ **Exxon** 24 Hrs.
Self-serve, mini-mart, cash &
credit cards, diesel, restrooms,
phone, ice.

⑰ **USA Gas** 24 Hrs.
Self-serve, large mini-mart,
cash only, RV pump-out,
restrooms with handicapped
access, phone, picnic tables.

⑱ **Arco am/pm** 24 Hrs.
Self-serve, mini-mart, cash &
cash-machine cards, restrooms
with handicapped access,
phone, lots of parking.

⑲ **Blaine Gas** 24 Hrs.
Self-serve, mini-mart, cash &
credit cards, restrooms, phone.

Restaurants

② **Vista Rib Steak &
Spaghetti House** $$
11am-1am, 7 days. Full &
counter service with take-out
available. Cash & credit cards
& checks. American and Italian
menu, specializing in burgers
and pizza.

⑤ **Costa Azul** $$
11am-10pm Tues-Thurs, 11am-
11pm Fri-Sun, Closed Mon.
Full-service restaurant. Cash &
credit cards & checks. Mexican
menu. Full bar. On-street
parking.

⑩ **El Sombrero** $$
4pm-9pm Mon-Thurs, 4pm-
10pm Fri-Sat, 12pm-9pm Sun.
Full-service restaurant. Cash &
credit cards. Mexican menu.
Full bar.

Fast Food

① **Subway**
⑫ **Denny's**

Lodging

⑮ **Northwoods Motel** ☺☺
$$ (206) 332-5603 Cash &
credit cards. Commercial
discount & weekly rates
available. Non-smoking rooms
available. All rooms have tub
with shower. Phones, cable TV,
exercise area, spa, outdoor pool.
Fax available. No pets.

Other

⑦ **Police Station**

⑧ **Peace Arch Park**
  • Picnic areas
  • Restrooms

⑨ **Pac Can Duty-Free Store**
  • 8am-9pm Mon-Thurs,
    8am-10pm Fri-Sun

Peace Arch Park straddles the US/Canadian border. At the center is the Peace Arch, a 67-foot structure with one column in each country to symbolize Canadian-US friendship. The Peace Arch is surrounded by colorful, well-tended gardens and the Park has a beautiful view of the harbor.

Peace Arch Park is a wonderful place for a picnic or stroll, whether or not you pass through customs to the other side. If you're just visiting the Park, you can reach it from Blaine (see Exit 276).

Wintertime at the Peace Arch on the US/Canadian border at Blaine.

Index: Fast Food

Note: Fast food restaurants might be free-standing or located in a Mall. Check the Fast Food and Mall Listings for the exact location. Numbers are the Exit numbers where the restaurant can be found.

7-11 Hoagy's Corner: 179

A

A&W Hamburgers: 3
Aleko's Pizza: 172
Alfy's Pizza: 181, 186, 189
Andree's Coffee House: 82
Arby's: 82, 102, 108, 132, 137, 162, 163, 173, 177, 181, 199, 227, 252
Aurora Teriyaki: 174

B

Bagel Factory: 252
Baskin-Robbins: 3, 103, 108, 122, 137, 149, 169, 171, 173, 181, 192, 253
BBQ on a Bun: 169
Benji's Fish & Chips: 167
Bento Teriyaki: 179
Bergsma Gallery & Cafe: 253
Big Scoop: 227
Big Tom's: 103
Bill & Bea's Burgers: 82
Boehm Candy Kitchen: 170
Boomer's Drive-Inn: 252
Bosley's BBQ: 206
Brewery City Pizza: 102, 109
Burger & Shake Shop: 122
Burger Bar: 30
Burger Box: 137
Burger King: 4, 7, 39, 82, 102, 109, 129, 132, 137, 142, 143, 149, 153, 162, 163, 167, 169, 174, 175, 181, 186, 199, 227, 229, 252, 256, 275
Burgermaster: 88
Burgerville: 1C, 1D, 4, 7, 21, 82
By's Burgers: 163

C

California Burgers: 182
Catlin's: 82, 102
Countryside Donut House: 173

D

Dairy Bar Burgers: 77
Dairy Queen: 1D, 21, 88, 105A 108, 111, 127, 129, 135, 142, 186, 189, 199, 227, 254, 262, 275
Daly's Drive In: 168A
Darn Good Pizza: 174
Dave's Burgers: 181
Denny's: 1C, 4, 39, 76, 82, 109, 125, 128, 137, 142, 143, 153, 156, 163, 167, 173, 177, 181, 186, 193, 208, 227, 252, 256, 276
Domino's Pizza: 123, 168A
Drive-In Burgers: 59
Dunkin' Donuts: 149, 174

E

El Taco Grande: 21
Elo's Philly Grill: 163
Espresso & Deli: 109

F

Family Donut: 173
Figaro's Pizza: 3, 107
Fish Bowl Fish & Chips: 175
Flynn's Cafe: 163
Frankfurter, The: 171, 173
Frisko Freeze: 127

Fast Food

G

Georgetown Bakery & Cafe: 162
Godfather's Pizza: 82, 108, 143, 151, 153, 175, 177, 182, 189, 227, 252, 256
Grant's Drive-In: 262

H

Haagen Dazs: 171
Happy Teriyaki: 132, 153, 181
Hawaii BBQ: 181
Hero at Large: 108
Home Plate Deli: 206

I

I Love Sushi: 167
International House of Pancakes: 129, 143, 169, 181
Ivar's Seafood: 127, 143, 169, 174, 192
Izzy's Pizza: 107

J

Jack in the Box: 76, 102, 105B, 108, 129, 133, 136, 147, 156, 163, 169, 172, 181, 183, 189, 194, 199, 206, 227, 230, 255
Jacques Deli: 183
Jane's Cafe: 174
JBob's In-&-Out: 72

K

Katie's Deli & Teriyaki: 182
Kauai Family Rest.: 162
Kentucky Fried Chicken: 4, 102, 122, 125, 137, 174, 181, 186, 192, 194, 227

Kidd Valley Hamburgers: 175
Kiko Teriyaki: 147
Kim's Deli: 162
King's Table: 192
Konich's Teriyaki: 149

L

Le Donut: 132
Little Caesar's Pizza: 4, 82, 175, 253
Little Tokyo Teriyaki: 129, 132
Lumberjack Pizza: 21

M

McDonald's: 3, 39, 72, 82, 102, 105B, 108, 111, 127, 132, 137, 142, 143, 149, 153, 162, 163, 173, 177, 181, 186, 192, 199, 227, 230, 252, 254, 256
Madeleine's Drive-Thru: 125
Madrid's Espresso: 107
Meal Time Burger: 149
Mrs. Beesley's: 59
My Kitchen Bakery: 186

N

Nippon: 182

O

Olympia Pizza House: 206
Once Upon a Tea Time Deli: 30
Oskar's German Deli: 108

P

Pacific Pizza: 76
Pagliacci Pizza: 168A
Pancake Haus: 173
Papa Pete's Pizza Parlor: 49

Fast Food

P

Pastry Cafe: 182
Pazzo's Pizza: 168A
Pietro's Pizza: 4, 108
Pizza Factory: 230
Pizza Hut: 3, 82, 102, 149, 175, 181, 186, 253
Pizza Time: 171
Popeye's: 142
Port of Subs: 179, 255
Poseidon Fish & Chips: 162

Q

Quarterback Pub: 252
Quick's Burgers: 82
Quick Fix: 167

R

R.E.freshers: 253
Ragamuffin's Deli: 3
Rax: 189
Round Table Pizza: 4, 7, 129, 173, 227, 252, 255
Royal Fork Buffet: 199, 227

S

Sandwich Aisle: 181
Saucy's Pizza: 230
Shakey's: 227
Shari's: 39, 82, 107, 109, 129, 142, 256
Sizzler: 107, 127, 153, 173, 182, 256
Skipper's: 3, 137, 149, 173, 181, 182, 186, 227, 254
Smokey's Pizza: 3
Sno-King Bakery: 177
Spud Fish & Chips: 171
Starbucks Coffee: 129, 147, 173, 189, 227, 252, 255

Steakburger: 3
Sub Shop: 82, 123, 173, 229
Subway: 3, 21, 82, 102, 122, 127, 130, 142, 147, 149, 153, 163, 168A, 169, 174, 177, 181, 183, 252, 276
Sunset Burgers: 255

T

TCBY Yogurt: 143, 182, 255
Taco Bandito: 49
Taco Bell: 3, 7, 39, 82, 109, 122, 129, 132, 147, 149, 163, 186, 227, 255
Taco Time: 3, 107, 127, 132, 143, 153, 162, 173, 175, 181, 183, 186, 199, 206, 253, 256
Take 'n Bake Pizza: 206
Teriyaki Bowl: 229
Teriyaki Plus: 163, 169, 173, 177, 186
Teriyaki Time: 153
Toshi's Teriyaki: 177
Tukwila Deli: 156
Tuxedo's Cafe: 158

W

Wendy's: 4, 82, 108, 132, 137, 143, 153, 199, 229
Westernco Donut: 163, 169, 177
Whimpy's Burgers: 21
Winchell's Donuts: 108, 169, 227
Winchell's Eatery: 255
WOKS Deli: 162

Y

Yak's Deli: 163
Yukio's Teriyaki: 107
Yumiko Teriyaki: 168A
Yummy Teriyaki: 186

Lodging

7 West Motel: 49

A

Aloha Motel: 252
Arlington Motor Inn: 208

B

Bay City Motor Inn: 252
Bell Northwoods Motel: 252
Best Western Executel: 143
Best Western Ferryman's Inn: 4
Best Western Heritage Inn: 256
Best Western Lakeway Inn: 253
Best Western Landmark Inn: 181
Best Western Motor Inn: 227
Best Western Tacoma Inn: 128
Best Western Tumwater Inn: 102
Budget Inn: 127

C

Capitol Inn: 109
Carriage Inn: 105B
Cascade Motel: 76
Century Motel: 149
Coachman Inn: 252
Cocusa Motel: 230
Colonial Motel: 125
Columbia Inn Motel: 30
Comfort Inn: 7, 39, 109, 137, 189
Cotton Tree Inn: 227
Cypress Inn: 186

D

Day's Inn: 129, 136
Doubletree Inn: 153
Doubletree Suites: 153

E

Eastlake Inn: 168A
Econo-Lodge: 136
Embassy Suites: 181
Everett Pacific Hotel: 193
Executive Inn: 137

F

Ferryman's Inn: 82
Fort Motel: 1B
Fort Lewis Motel: 125

G

Georgetown Inn: 162
Glacier Motel: 136

H

Hampton Inn: 258
Hansen's Motel: 21
Hillside Motel: 218
Holiday Inn: 158, 186
Holiday Inn Express: 181
Home Motel: 125
Hometel Inn: 136
Howard Johnson Lodge: 128
Huntley Inn: 82

K

Key Motel: 252
King's Inn: 137
King's Arms Motel: 149

Lodging

L

La Quinta Inn: 135
Lake Shore Motel: 81
Lakeside Motel: 21
Lakewood Lodge: 125
Lewis River Inn: 21

M

Mac's Motel: 252
Madigan Motel: 125
Mariott Courtyard: 153
Mark II Motel: 230
Max Ivor Motel: 162
Meany Tower Hotel: 169
Motel 6: 39, 82, 129, 137, 151, 152, 186, 252
Mt. St. Helens Motel: 49

N

Nendel's Inn: 193
Nendel's Suites: 3
New Best Inn: 149
Northwoods Motel: 276

P

Park Motel: 82, 252
Peppertree Motel & RV Park: 81
Pony Soldier Motor Inn: 76

R

Ramada Inn: 133, 173, 189, 252
Red Lion Inn: 39
Residence Inn: 167, 182
Riverside Motel: 82
Roadrunner: 142
Rose Garden Motel: 125

Rothem Inn: 128
Royal Coachman Inn: 137

S

Scandia Motel: 21
Scottish Lodge: 262
Shamrock Motel: 258
Shangri-La Motel: 253
Sherwood Inn: 128
Shilo Inn: 1B, 7, 129
Silver Cloud Inn: 156, 181
Smokey Point Motor Inn: 206
Sterling Motor Inn: 230
Super 8: 109, 142

T

Timberland Motel: 49
Towne & Country Motor Inn: 227
Traveler's Inn: 136, 256
Travelodge: 128, 193, 227
Tulalip Inn: 199
Tulip Inn: 227
Tyee Hotel: 102

U

University Inn: 169
University Plaza Hotel: 169

V

Vagabond Inn: 127
Val-u Inn Motel: 253
Value Inn: 4
Village Motor Inn: 199

W

West Winds Motel: 227
Western Inn: 127
Woodlander Inn: 21

Parks & Recreation

Restaurants

Note: Restaurants might be free-standing or located in a Mall. Check the Restaurant and Mall Listings for the exact location. Numbers are the Exit numbers where the restaurant can be found.

13th Ave. Pub & Eatery: 183
41st St. Bar & Grill: 192

A

Adolfo's: 163
Andy's Diner: 163
Applebee's: 181
Ashiya: 183
Asia Garden: 181
Asian Palace: 174
Austin's Rio Cafe: 227
Azteca: 132, 153, 173, 179, 182, 189

B

Bamboo Inn: 252
Barnaby's: 173
Bells: 172
Benjamin's: 167
Billy McHale's: 127, 143, 182
BK's Kitchen: 149
Black Angus: 143, 181, 252
Blockhouse: 149
Bob's Burgers & Brew: 262
Buzz Inn Steak House: 177, 189, 192, 206

C

Calico Family Restaurant: 256
Calico Inn Pancake House: 252
Calzone's: 129
Casa Mia: 105B, 109
Casa Ramos: 82
Cascade Pizza Inn: 227
Cattle Company: 1B
Cedars on Brooklyn: 169
Chandler's Crab House: 167
China City: 171
China Coin: 153
China Doll: 193

China Dragon: 82
China First: 169
China Passage: 179
China Town: 128
China Wok: 230
Chinese Delight: 181
Ching Ha: 123
Choi's Dynasty: 4
Cranberry Tree: 227
Christie's: 137
Chuck-E-Cheese: 130, 181
Coco's: 177, 181
Columbia Inn: 30
Cookhouse, The: 177
Cooper's NW Ale House: 171
Copperfield's: 128
Costa Azul: 276
Country Cousin: 82
Country Harvest: 181
Country House Cafe: 59
Country Junction: 14, 111
Crystal Palace II: 105B
Cucina!Cucina!: 132, 153, 167

D

DaHaRi Oriental Buffet: 127
Daimonji: 162
Don's: 199
Dragon Inn: 227
Dragon King: 4
Drumman's: 227
Duke's: 167
Duke's Chowder House: 167

E

El Cazador: 230
El Presidente: 1B
El Serape: 108
El Sombrero: 276

Restaurants

E

El Torito: 130, 181
Eleni's: 253
Elmer's: 129, 182
Eng's China Kitchen: 181

F

Falls Terrace: 103
Farm Boy: 95
Fresh Choice: 143
Fryday's: 252

G

GA Maxwell's: 199
Galeria's: 168A
Galley, The: 230
Galloping Gertie's: 122
Gaspare's Ristorante Italiano: 171
Gikan #5 Teriyaki: 151
Gourmet City: 174
Grand Peking: 143
Grazie Caffe Italiano: 153
Great China: 181
Great River: 186
Great Wall: 262

H

Hacienda: 88
Happy Teriyaki V: 102
Hawk's Prairie Inn: 111
Hilander: 39
Himalaya: 170
Hong Kong Express: 153

I

Ichi Teriyaki: 143
Ike's: 162
India House: 169
India Palace: 174
Iron Skillet: 102
Italo: 175

J

Jim's Diner: 102
Johnny's at Fife: 137
Jollie's: 9

K

Kalama Cafe: 30
Kamon: 167
Kayak Grill: 167
Keg, The: 169, 182, 252
King Solomon: 81
King's Chinese: 171
King's Palace: 137
Kings III: 177
Kit Carson Coffee Shop: 76
Kostalee's Family Pasta & Pizza: 181
Krackles Grill: 9
Kyodai: 177

L

La Casa Real: 136
La Palma II: 108
Las Coronas: 206
Las Margaritas: 175, 199
Las Palomas: 149
Latitude 47: 167
Leslie's: 125
Little Beijing: 174
Little Red Barn: 88
Luna-Rossa: 171

M

Macheezmo Mouse: 181
Mama's Bake Shop: 4
Mandarin House: 109
Marie Callender's: 173
Marilyn's: 135
Mason Jar: 103
Max Dale's: 227
Mayflower of China: 153
Mazatlan: 127

Restaurants

M

Mi Mexico: 256
Mi Pueblo: 256
Mitzel's: 109, 129, 137, 186, 227, 256
Miyabi: 153
Mongolian Grill: 129
Mr. D's: 82
Mustard Seed: 68

N

Neon Moon: 181
New Hong Kong: 4
New Peking: 171, 193
Newaukum Valley Restaurant & Bakery: 71
Nickelby's: 102
North China: 173, 255
North Gardens: 189

O

Oak Tree: 21
O'Brien Turkey House: 208
O'Houlie's Pub: 179
Olive Garden: 129, 181, 189
Omni: 152
Opus Too Grill: 167
Orchid: 189
Oriental Garden: 111

P

Pacific Highway Diner: 142
Paraiso: 206
Pegasus: 135
Peking: 227
Peking House: 176
Peper's 49er: 49
Peppermill: 81
Petosa's: 193, 206
PioPio's: 182
Pizza Experience: 137

Pizza Roma: 128
Plaza Jalisco: 79
Poodle Dog, The: 137

R

Randy's: 158
Rasa Malaysia: 171
Red Coral: 108
Red Lobster: 129, 143, 181
Red Robin: 132, 143, 153, 173, 182, 189, 229, 256
Restover: 99
Reunion: 3
Rib 'n Beef: 252
Rib Eye: 72
Ricky's: 253
Ristorante Toscana: 169
Ritz Diner: 153
Rose Tree: 49
Rose's Hiway Inn: 147

S

Sadighi's: 253
Sakura: 4
Sea Galley: 262
Serafina's: 168A
Shanghai: 105A
Slo-Pitch Pub & Eatery: 255
Smiley's Pizza: 252
Spiffy's: 68
Stage Coach Inn: 7
South Pacific: 103
Sunlight Cafe: 170

T

T.G.I. Friday's: 132, 167
TK: 128
Taki: 181
Taste of India: 256
Tee-Dee's Pie House: 3
Thai House: 256

Restaurants

T

Thai Hut: 173
Thai Terrace: 179
Than Ying Thai Cuisine: 168A
Tiny's Burgerhouse: 114
Tony Roma's: 130, 153, 173, 181
Totem Pole: 4
Truck City Truck Stop: 225
Tsuruya: 181
Turning Point: 136

V

Village: 199
Vista Rib Steak, & Spaghetti House: 276

W

Wanza: 170
Wayne's: 206
Weller's Chalet: 208
White Spot: 255
Winner's: 153
Winter Kitchen: 81

Y

Yankee Diner: 181

Z

Zack's: 230
Zoopa: 153

RV Parks

99 Mobile Lodge RV Park: 7

C

Camp Kalama Campground & RV Park: 32
Cedars RV Park: 46

F

Ferndale Campground: 263

G

Good Sam Park (at Shell Station): 68

K

KOA Campground: 236

M

Mermac Store & RV Park: 52

N

Nisqually Plaza RV Park: 114

P

Peppertree Motel & RV Park: 81

R

River Oaks RV Park: 59
Rotary Riverside Park: 82
RV Park: 57

S

Seattle South KOA Campground: 152
Smokey Point RV Park: 206

T

Thousand Trails Campground: 236

Service Stations

7-11: 102, 151, 157, 169, 174, 177, 179, 186, 206

A

Alger Pit Stop: 240
AMMEX Duty Free Shop: 276
Arco: 2, 4, 14, 21, 39, 49, 68, 76, 82, 88, 103, 108, 111, 122, 124, 127, 128, 129, 132, 135, 137, 142, 143, 147, 153, 163, 170, 172, 173, 174, 177, 179, 181, 182, 183, 186, 189, 192, 199, 206, 208, 230, 252, 260, 266, 276
Arlington Fuel Stop: 208

B

Blaine Gas: 276
Bode's Truck Stop: 71
BP: 4, 14, 30, 59, 72, 77, 102, 109, 111, 124, 127, 128, 135, 137, 143, 151, 152, 156, 157, 163, 169, 171, 172, 173, 177, 181, 186, 192, 193, 199, 202, 208, 231, 252, 254, 255, 258, 262, 275

C

Cenex Gas: 229
Chevron: 1C, 21, 39, 82, !02, 105B, 107, 111, 128, 142, 151, 153, 162, 169, 172, 173, 174, 177, 181, 183, 186, 193, 199, 202, 208, 227, 230, 231, 250, 252, 254, 276
Circle K: 14, 147
Citgo: 3, 7, 107
Classic Gas: 255
Country Pump: 189

E

Express Way Food Store: 7
Exxon: 63, 227, 230, 258, 262, 275, 276

F

Flying J Truck Plaza: 136
Fred's Discount Tires: 88
Frontier Foods: 101

G

Gas Mini Mart: 215

J

Jackpot Food Mart: 77, 255

L

Liberty Gas: 162, 163

M

Main Street Astro: 2
Minit Mart: 21

P

Pacific Auto Store: 40
Pink Pantry: 176

R

Restover Truck Stop: 99

Service Stations

S

Shell: 4, 9, 21, 39, 68, 72, 81, 108, 114, 274, 276
Smokey Point Mini Mart: 206
Speedway Grocery: 88
Sunset Self-Serve Gas: 255

T

Texaco: 3, 4, 16, 21, 27, 39, 49, 57, 68, 79, 81, 82, 88, 102, 103, 107, 108, 109, 111, 114, 127, 128, 130, 132, 133, 136, 137, 142, 143, 147, 149, 156, 162, 163, 164B, 169, 170, 173, 176, 177, 179, 181, 183, 186, 189, 192, 194, 199, 206, 208, 212, 221, 227, 230, 246, 252, 253, 254, 256, 262, 263, 275, 276
Trail Mart: 7
Truck City Truck Stop: 225

U

Unocal 76: 4, 7, 108, 125, 156, 167, 169, 181, 183, 199, 206, 226, 227, 252, 254, 256, 276
USA: 181, 229, 253, 276

Shopping Malls

Shopping Malls

O

Olson's Plaza: 175
Olympia Square: 107
Outlet Market Place: 82

P

Pacific Edge Outlet Center:
 229
Pacific Linen Plaza: 182
Park Way Plaza: 153
Pavilion Mall: 153
Plaza 99: 3
Puget Park Mall: 186

R

Rainier Place Mall: 132
Riverway Plaza: 39
Ross Olympia Square: 107

S

Salmon Creek Plaza: 7
Sea-Tac Mall: 143
Sea-Tac Village Mall: 143
Sehome Village Mall: 252
Silo Plaza: 182
Smokey Point Mall: 206
Smokey Point Plaza: 206
South Sound Center: 108
Southcenter Mall: 153
Southcenter Plaza: 153
Sunset Square: 255

T

Tacoma Mall: 130
Tacoma Place Mall: 129
Tacoma South Center: 129
Target Plaza: 182
Terrace Village: 179
Three Rivers Mall: 39
Toys-R-Us Mall: 153

W

Wood World Mall: 181
Woodland Mall: 21

Order Blank

To: Bryce Publications
P.O. Box 23365
Federal Way, WA 98093-0365
1-800-662-1437

WASHINGTON

Please send me _____ copies of the book *I-5 Travel Guide* for *Washington*.

Ship To:
Name:_____

Address:_____

City:_____State:_____Zip:_____

Daytime Telephone: (   ) _____

Total Enclosed:
$_____   for _____copies at $14.95 each ($18.95 Canadian)

$_____   Tax (Washington residents add $1.23 per book for
              State sales tax)

$_____   Add $2.00 postage and handling for the first book,
              $1.00 for each additional book.

$_____   TOTAL ENCLOSED

Payment must accompany order. All orders are sent book rate.

Payment:
( ) Here is my check, payable to **Bryce Publications**

Please charge my ( ) Visa or ( ) Mastercard

Card number:_____Exp. date:___/___

Signature:_____

For credit card orders only, order by fax or phone between 8am
and 6pm PST by calling 1-800-662-1437.